MW01148526

No Grid Survival

Projects Book

The DIY Guide to Self-Sufficiency and Off-Grid Living | Survival Kit for a Safe Home, Power, Food Supply, First Aid & Other Prepper Hacks to Survive Any Crisis or Recession

Grant Miller

Table of contents

Introduction 6

Chapter 1: Understanding Off-the-Grid Living 8

    1.1   What Does It Mean to Live Off-the-Grid? 8

    1.2   Why Go Off-Grid? 8

    1.3   Is Off-the-Grid Living Right for You? 9

    1.4   Benefits and Challenges of Off-the-Grid Living 10

Chapter 2: Essential Preparations 14

    2.1 Assessing Your Needs and Resources 14

    2.2 Developing a Comprehensive Plan 15

    2.3 Setting Realistic Goals 16

    2.4 Financial Planning for Self-Sufficiency 17

    2.5 Securing the Right Location and Land 18

    2.6 Adapting to Different Environments and Climates 19

    2.7 Legal and Regulatory Considerations 21

Chapter 3: Off-the-Grid Shelter Project 23

    3.1 Planning and Designing Your Off-Grid Home 23

    3.2 Building or Choosing Suitable Shelter Options 25

    3.3 Energy-Efficient and Sustainable Design Techniques 28

    3.4 DIY Off-the-Grid Shelter Projects (Building Your Shelter) 30

    3.5 Heating and Cooling Solutions Without Reliance On the Grid 33

Chapter 4: Off-the-Grid Power Solutions 35

    4.1 Solar Energy 36

    4.2 Wind and Hydro Power Options 41

    4.3 Micro-Hydro System to Generate Electricity 43

    4.4 Energy Storage, Management, and Conservation 44

    4.5 Backup Power Systems 44

Chapter 5: Water Management 45

    5.1 Sourcing and Treating Water 45

    5.2 Techniques for Rainwater Harvesting and Groundwater Sourcing 46

    5.3 DIY Water Filtration System and Purification 47

5.4 Water Pump with Solar Panels...48

    5.5 Water Conservation and Storage Solutions 49

    5.6 Off-Grid Hot Water...50

Chapter 6: Off-the-Grid Food Production and Preservation 52

    6.1 Sustainable Food Production 52

    6.2 Food Preservation Techniques..57

    6.3 Effective Food Storage...59

    6.4 Advanced Food Production Strategies 62

Chapter 7: Off-the-Grid Security and Self-Defense.....................................66

    7.1 Securing Your Property 66

    7.2 Emergency Response Planning 67

    7.3 Basic Self-Defense Techniques...69

Chapter 8: Essential Skills for Off-the-Grid Living 73

    8.1 First Aid and Medical Skills 73

    8.2 Survival Skills 76

    8.3 DIY Repair Skills 77

Chapter 9: Off-the-Grid Transport and Communication...............................80

    9.1 Off-Grid Transportation..80

    9.2 Off-Grid Communication...84

Chapter 10: Thriving Off-the-Grid 88

    10.1 Overcoming Challenges..88

    10.2 Finding Fulfillment in Self-Sufficiency 90

    10.3 Tips for Long-Term Sustainability..91

Conclusion 94

Copyright © [2024] by Grant Miller

All rights reserved. No part of this book should be reproduced, distributed, or transmitted in any form or by any means, including photocopying, recording, or other electronic or mechanical methods, without the prior written permission of the publisher, except in the case of brief quotations embodied in critical reviews and certain other noncommercial uses permitted by copyright law.

About the Author

Grant Miller is an outdoor enthusiast, who's passionate about exploring the natural world and mastering the art of self-sufficiency. While growing up, he loved to travel and camping.

He has a wealth of experience in hiking, camping, and bushcraft. Also, Grant has honed his skills in surviving and thriving off-grid. His adventures have taken him to notable places like Alaska's Interior Wilderness, Utah's Canyonlands, The Everglades, Florida, and many more, where he's learned invaluable lessons about resilience, resourcefulness, and the importance of sustainable living.

His love for the outdoors goes beyond a hobby—it has become his lifestyle. He believes in the power of nature to teach us profound lessons and inspire us to live more intentionally. With his writing, Grant aims to share his knowledge, insights, and passion for no-grid survival with readers around the world.

Introduction

We seem to worry over things that are out of our control. And whine over the ones we can control. Also, you don't need to wait for an emergency before seeking a solution; you should prepare ahead of time. That's why you need to equip yourself with survival skills, especially off-grid ones.

Can you imagine a world where we can't fully rely on the usual power sources or stores for our needs? That's where "No Grid Survival Projects Book" steps in! It's a guidebook that teaches you how to be self-sufficient and live off the grid.

It's not just about surviving tough times; it's also about being ready for anything that might come your way, like a crisis or a recession. This reminds me of the story of a teenager, Josh.

Josh was a young boy with an insatiable curiosity and a passion for learning about survival and solving problems. While he was growing up, he was always eager to explore new ideas and discover innovative ways to overcome challenges.

Fortunately for him, he had an uncle who shared his enthusiasm for both indoor and outdoor skills. His uncle was a true survivalist, knowledgeable in everything from setting up campfires to building sturdy shelters and growing food sustainably.

One day, Josh visited his uncle's cabin in the woods. Then, he found one of his uncle's books on the shelf. This book talks about how one can survive off the grid. He was intrigued by the title. So, he eagerly flipped through the pages, absorbing every word like a sponge.

Under his uncle's guidance, Josh started applying the lessons from the book in real life. Together, they transformed a patch of land near the cabin into a flourishing garden, using eco-friendly techniques to nurture plants and vegetables.

As Josh read more pages and chapters in this book, he learned essential survival skills such as setting up solar panels for power, creating makeshift tools, and administering basic first aid. His uncle's mentorship and the knowledge from the book inspired Josh's passion for self-sufficiency and preparedness.

A power outage hit his area of Josh's residence, plunging the cabin into darkness on one stormy night. But thanks to his newfound skills and the solar panels they had installed, they remained comfortably lit and warm, unaffected by the blackout.

Josh's journey didn't just end there. He continued to hone his skills and share his knowledge with others.

That's Josh's story, and you can even do better than he did with "No Grid Survival Handbook Projects. This book will teach you how to make your home safe and strong, so you can feel secure no matter what happens. Also, you'll discover cool tricks to get power without depending on big companies, grow your food, and even handle emergencies like a pro with first aid skills.

So, if you're curious about living off-grid or just want to be super prepared, this book is your ultimate guide to an awesome, self-sufficient life! You're about to learn essential survival skills. I believe you will be glad you did.

Ensure you leave your honest review once you're done reading this book.

I wish you good luck and the very best.

Chapter 1: Understanding Off-the-Grid Living

The very first step to living off the grid is to understand what it entails. Rest assured, you will learn what it means to live off the grid, exploring the motivations, challenges, and rewards of this captivating lifestyle. From generating your electricity to harvesting water and growing your food, off-the-grid living is about embracing alternative methods and reducing reliance on traditional utilities. But why do people choose this path? What considerations should you keep in mind? And most importantly, is off-the-grid living the right choice for you?

In this chapter, I can assure you that you will unravel the essence of off-the-grid living, offering insights and perspectives that will empower you to make informed decisions about your journey towards a more sustainable and fulfilling lifestyle. We have 4 subchapters that will help do justice to understanding this concept. Now, let's get into the details

1.1   What Does It Mean to Live Off-the-Grid?

As an enthusiast and survivalist, you should understand that living off the grid is about embracing a simpler, more sustainable lifestyle that prioritizes self-reliance, resourcefulness, and a closer connection to nature. So, this whole concept means choosing to be self-sufficient and independent from mainstream utilities and infrastructure. In essence, this lifestyle involves generating your electricity, collecting and managing your water supply, and producing your food without relying on public services.

Below are the key aspects of living off the grid:
- Energy Independence
- Water Management
- Food Production
- Waste Management
- Reduced Reliance on External Systems

You will know more about these key aspects in the coming chapters.

1.2   Why Go Off-Grid?

This question should be addressed properly. It will help you understand the essence of living off the grid. People choose this lifestyle for lots of reasons. Now, let's check some of these reasons out.

First, it's great for the environment. When you use solar panels or wind turbines for power, you're not burning fossil fuels that harm the planet. Also, you save money in the long run because you're not paying utility bills. Being off-grid also makes you more independent. You produce your food, manage your water, and handle waste on your own. This self-sufficiency is handy during emergencies or when there are disruptions in city services. Living off the grid can also bring a simpler, and less hectic life. You're away from city noise and surrounded by nature, which can be peaceful and good for your mental health. It's also a chance to learn and pass down traditional skills like gardening, preserving food, and building things. Kids growing up off-grid get a unique education and learn to appreciate nature and hard work. Lastly, off-grid communities often have a strong sense of togetherness. People help each other out, share resources, and work together on projects that benefit everyone.

Therefore, going off-grid isn't just about saving money or being eco-friendly. It's about living a more self-reliant, simpler life that's good for you and the planet.

1.3 Is Off-the-Grid Living Right for You?

The decision to embrace off-the-grid living depends on your unique priorities, values, and lifestyle preferences. Let's explore some examples to help you make an informed decision:

❖ **Location and Accessibility**: To whether off-the-grid living is right for you, you can consider the location of your potential off-grid property. If you prefer remote, secluded areas with abundant natural resources, such as forests or farmland, off-grid living may align with your preferences. On the other hand, if you value proximity to urban amenities and easy access to healthcare, schools, and shopping, you might find off-grid living challenging.

❖ **Lifestyle Preferences:** If you enjoy a simpler, more self-sufficient lifestyle and crave closer connections with nature, off-grid living could be a good fit. For example, if you love gardening, raising animals, and being outdoors, living off-grid will allow you to fully embrace these activities.

❖ **Social and Community Considerations:** You should think about your social connections and community preferences. Off-grid living can be isolating for some of you, especially if you thrive on social interactions or rely heavily on community services. Conversely, if you value independence, privacy, and a strong sense of community within off-grid neighborhoods, this lifestyle may suit you well.

❖ **Budget and Financial Considerations:** Off-grid living requires an initial investment in renewable energy systems, water collection methods, and sustainable infrastructure. If you have the financial resources to set up and maintain these systems, such as purchasing solar panels or digging a well, off-grid living can be feasible. However, if you're on a tight budget or prefer a more cost-effective lifestyle, staying connected to public utilities may be more practical.

❖ **Energy and Resource Management:** It is also important you evaluate your willingness and ability to manage energy and resources efficiently. Off-grid living involves monitoring energy usage, conserving water, and implementing waste management strategies. For instance, if you're committed to reducing your environmental impact and enjoy hands-on resource management, off-grid living offers opportunities for sustainable practices.

❖ **Skills and Preparedness:** You must assess your skills and preparedness for off-grid living challenges. Are you comfortable with DIY projects, troubleshooting renewable energy systems, and handling basic maintenance tasks? Off-grid living requires a hands-on approach and adaptability to unexpected situations. For example, if you enjoy learning new skills, problem-solving, and embracing a more self-reliant lifestyle, off-grid living can be rewarding.

1.4 Benefits and Challenges of Off-the-Grid Living

This subchapter is quite straightforward. However, I believe it will be great to explain the benefits and challenges of living off-the-grid in isolation. Doing this will help drive home points. Are you ready? Let's get into it.

Benefits of Off-the-Grid Living

Living off the grid comes with a range of benefits that might appeal to you if you are seeking self-sufficiency, sustainability, and a deeper connection with nature.

Let's explore some of the key advantages of off-the-grid living:

➤ **Self-Sufficiency:** Off-gridders produce their food, manage water sources, and handle waste independently. This self-sufficiency fosters resilience, reduces reliance on external systems, and prepares individuals for emergencies or disruptions in city services.

➤ **Environmental Sustainability**: By relying on renewable energy sources like solar, wind, or hydroelectric power, off-gridders reduce their carbon footprint and minimize environmental impact. This commitment to sustainability contributes to preserving natural resources and combating climate change.

➤ **Educational Opportunities**: Off-grid living provides unique educational opportunities, especially for children. They learn practical life skills, environmental stewardship, and the value of self-reliance, fostering a deeper understanding of sustainability and resilience.

➤ **Community and Collaboration**: Off-grid communities foster a strong sense of camaraderie, collaboration, and mutual support. Residents share resources, knowledge, and skills, creating tight-knit communities focused on sustainability, resilience, and collective well-being.

➤ **Closer Connection with Nature**: Living off the grid often means residing in natural settings with abundant wildlife, clean air, and scenic landscapes. This closer connection with nature promotes mental well-being, reduces stress, and encourages outdoor activities and exploration.

➤ **Energy Independence**: Off-grid living gives freedom from utility bills and power outages. Generating your electricity through solar panels or wind turbines means you're not at the mercy of grid disruptions or rising energy costs. This energy independence provides stability and financial savings over time.

➤ **Healthier Lifestyle**: Off-grid living encourages healthier lifestyle choices. Access to fresh, homegrown food promotes a nutritious diet, while the active, outdoor-oriented lifestyle enhances physical fitness and overall well-being.

➤ **Cost Savings:** While the initial setup costs for off-grid systems can be significant, the long-term savings outweigh these expenses. Without monthly utility bills and with the potential to grow your food, off-grid living can lead to considerable cost savings over time.

➤ **Minimal Environmental Impact:** Off-grid homes are often designed with eco-friendly features such as energy-efficient appliances, sustainable building materials, and water conservation systems. This minimal environmental impact aligns with conservation efforts and sustainable living practices.

➤ **Personal Freedom and Fulfillment:** Ultimately, off-the-grid living offers a sense of personal freedom, fulfillment, and purpose. It allows individuals to live in alignment with their values, reduce their environmental impact, and create a lifestyle that prioritizes simplicity, self-sufficiency, and harmony with nature.

Challenges of Off-the-Grid Living

As living off-the-grid has a lot of amazing advantages, you should understand that it also comes with its fair share of challenges. Let's explore some of the key challenges associated with off-the-grid living:

➤ **Learning Curve and Adaptability**: Transitioning to off-grid living requires a learning curve and adaptability to new technologies, skills, and lifestyle changes. So, you must be willing to learn about energy management, sustainable practices, and self-sufficiency while adapting to the realities of off-grid living.

➤ **Initial Setup Costs:** The upfront investment required for setting up off-grid systems like solar panels, wind turbines, water collection systems, and sustainable infrastructure is usually challenging. These initial costs can be substantial and might pose a barrier for enthusiasts and survivalists with limited financial resources.

➤ **Limited Energy and Water Capacity:** Chances are that off-grid homes will have limited energy and water capacity compared to grid-connected properties. Therefore, you have to be careful while managing energy usage, especially during periods of low sunlight or wind, and conserving water to avoid shortages during dry seasons or droughts.

➤ **Weather-Dependent Energy Generation:** Renewable energy sources like solar and wind power are weather-dependent. Cloudy days or calm winds can impact energy production, requiring alternative strategies or backup power sources during periods of low energy generation.

➤ **Water Availability and Quality:** Off-grid living relies on harvested rainwater, wells, or natural water sources. Ensuring a consistent supply of clean, potable water can be a challenge, particularly in arid regions or areas with limited water resources. Water quality and treatment also require attention to prevent contamination and ensure safe consumption.

➢ **Maintenance and Repairs:** To go off-grid, you must be ready for regular maintenance and occasional repairs of its systems.

That's not the end, you still have to monitor solar panels, check battery storage systems, maintain water filtration systems, and ensure the overall functionality of off-grid infrastructure. The responsibility for maintenance falls squarely on the homeowner, requiring time, effort, and sometimes specialized knowledge.

➢ **Isolation and Accessibility:** As expected, off-grid properties are located in remote or rural areas, which can lead to isolation and limited access to amenities, healthcare services, schools, and shopping. This isolation may pose challenges for you if you're accustomed to urban conveniences and social interactions.

➢ **Waste Management:** Proper waste management is essential in off-grid living to minimize environmental impact and maintain sanitation. You will need to implement effective waste disposal, recycling, and composting practices to manage household waste responsibly.

➢ **Regulatory and Legal Considerations:** Off-grid living may face regulatory and legal challenges related to building codes, zoning laws, permits for renewable energy installations, and water rights. To navigate these regulations and ensure compliance can be time-consuming and complex

➢ **Emergency Preparedness:** Off-grid living requires robust emergency preparedness plans. This includes provisions for backup power, water storage, first aid supplies, and communication methods in case of natural disasters, grid failures, or other emergencies.

Chapter 2: Essential Preparations

Did you know that preparations are crucial for your journey toward self-sufficiency, resilience, and a more sustainable lifestyle? And to adopt an off-grid lifestyle requires some intentional preparations from you. You should understand that doing this successfully can never be accidental. So, this section promises to educate you about the essential preparation of living off-the-grid.

Trust me, we will cover the basics of off-grid living and help you figure out what you need and what resources you have. Also, you'll learn how to make a solid plan, set achievable goals, and manage your finances for long-term success. In addition, you will explore how to spot the right location, adapt to different environments, and deal with legal stuff.

Now, let's dive in.

2.1 Assessing Your Needs and Resources

If you can assess your needs and resources comprehensively, it will be easier for you to prepare better, make informed decisions, and create a tailored off-grid plan that suits your lifestyle and goals. Also, you should understand that it's about figuring out what essentials you need to be self-sufficient and independent. To approach this assessment, below are some helpful tips:

❖ **Financial Resources:** Have you explored your financial options? You are required to do this. Also, you need to determine your budget for setting up off-grid systems, purchasing equipment, and ongoing maintenance. Living off the grid has its financial implications.

❖ **Skills and Knowledge:** Take stock of your skills and knowledge related to off-grid living. You must identify areas where you may need to learn new skills or seek assistance. Learn skills you know you can't do without.

❖ **Energy Needs:** You need to determine how much electricity you need daily and what appliances you'll be using. This helps in sizing your renewable energy systems like solar panels or wind turbines.

❖ **Water Requirements:** To live comfortably off-the-grid, you need to know the amount of water you use for drinking, cooking, cleaning, and irrigation if you plan on gardening. So, you should assess available water sources and their reliability.

❖ **Food Production:** It is necessary you evaluate your food needs and decide if you'll be growing vegetables, fruits, or raising animals. Also, you have to consider the space, climate, and resources required for sustainable food production.

❖ **Waste Management:** It is also expected of you to assess how you'll handle waste disposal, recycling, and composting. You need to plan for eco-friendly waste management systems.

❖ **Location Considerations:** It is also essential you evaluate potential off-grid locations based on factors like sunlight exposure for solar panels, water availability, soil quality for gardening, and accessibility to essential services.

2.2 Developing a Comprehensive Plan

Developing a comprehensive plan implies that you are mapping out your journey to off-grid living success. It involves creating a detailed roadmap that outlines how you'll achieve self-sufficiency and independence in all aspects of your life and well-being. So, here's how you can go about developing your plan:

➢ **Set Goals:** Ensure you define clear and achievable goals for your off-grid lifestyle. These could be as simple as; reducing your environmental impact, saving money on utilities, growing your food, or becoming more self-reliant.

➢ **Identify Priorities:** Essentially, you should determine what aspects of off-grid living are most important to you. Know what matters most and prioritize it. It could be renewable energy, water conservation, food production, or waste management.

➢ **Create a Timeline:** Without a timeline, your priorities and goals might not be achieved. So, you need to establish a timeline for implementing different components of your off-grid plan. This could include deadlines for installing solar panels, setting up a rainwater harvesting system, or starting a vegetable garden.

➢ **Budget and Financing:** Do the estimation of the costs associated with going off-grid, including equipment, materials, and ongoing maintenance. If required, you should develop a budget to explore your financing options.

➢ **Research and Education:** Educate yourself about off-grid living by researching best practices, techniques, and technologies. Also, you should attend workshops, join online communities, and learn from experienced off-gridders.

➤ **Plan for Contingencies:** As a survivalist, you must always anticipate challenges and setbacks by including contingency plans in your off-grid strategy. This could involve backup power sources, water storage solutions, or alternative food sources.

➤ **Monitor and Adjust:** You should review and evaluate your off-grid plan to track progress and make necessary adjustments regularly. Also, you need to be flexible and adapt to changing circumstances or new opportunities as a survivalist.

2.3 Setting Realistic Goals

When you set realistic goals as a survivalist, you set yourself up for success in your off-grid.

You must set achievable targets that align with your resources, capabilities, and timeline. To set realistic goals for your off-grid lifestyle, you should focus on the following:

- **Define Your Priorities:** You need to identify what matters most to you in off-grid living. Whether it is energy independence, sustainable food production, water conservation, or financial savings, ensure you prioritize your goals accordingly.

- **Be Specific and Measurable:** Make sure your goals are specific and measurable. Instead of a vague goal like "be more self-sufficient," aim for something concrete like "generate 60% of energy from renewable sources in 6 months."

- **Consider Resources and Constraints:** You should take stock of your resources, skills, and budget. To achieve this, you can set goals that are realistic within your means, considering factors like available land, climate, and regulatory requirements.

- **Break Goals into Milestones:** Most times, aiming to do a lot of huge tasks might lead to not doing anything at all. This is because you might get overwhelmed. So, you need to divide larger goals into smaller, manageable milestones. Doing this makes progress more tangible and allows for incremental achievements along the way.

- **Set Deadlines:** Ensure you assign deadlines to each goal and milestone and stick to them. This creates a sense of urgency and accountability, motivating you to stay on track and make continuous progress.

- **Factor in Flexibility:** It is also important you are flexible and adaptable in your goal-setting. Make sure you give room for adjustments based on changing circumstances, unexpected challenges, or new opportunities that may arise.

2.4 Financial Planning for Self-Sufficiency

When you strategically plan your finances, you can create a solid foundation for achieving self-sufficiency in off-grid living while ensuring long-term financial stability and resilience. Achieving this involves careful consideration of expenses, income sources, and long-term sustainability. To approach financial planning for self-sufficiency, below are some key steps:

- **Assess Current Finances:** You should start by evaluating your current financial situation. Ensure you calculate your monthly expenses, income, savings, and any existing debts or financial commitments.

- **Budgeting:** The next important thing you want to do is create a detailed budget that has all expenses related to off-grid living, such as renewable energy systems, water infrastructure, food production, waste management, maintenance, and emergency funds.

- **Cost Analysis:** Also, you need to research and estimate the costs associated with off-grid systems and infrastructure. This includes solar panels, batteries, wind turbines, water tanks, gardening supplies, and tools needed for self-sufficiency.

- **Income Sources:** You need a source of income to support your off-grid lifestyle. This could include part-time work, freelance opportunities, selling surplus produce or handmade goods, or investments that generate passive income. Just make sure you're making money.

- **Savings and Investments:** Another thing I will advise you to do is set aside savings or invest in assets that contribute to self-sufficiency. This could include purchasing land for food production, acquiring equipment for renewable energy, or investing in skills development for off-grid living.

- **Emergency Fund:** You should consider building an emergency fund to cover unexpected expenses or setbacks. Aim to have enough savings to sustain your off-grid lifestyle for many months in case of unforeseen circumstances.

- **Financial Goals:** While setting your financial goals, ensure they align with your off-grid objectives. These goals could be paying off debts, saving for specific projects or upgrades, or achieving financial independence through reduced reliance on external income sources.

- **Seek Professional Advice:** If you get caught up with all these financial hurdles, you can consider consulting with financial advisors or experts specializing in off-grid living. These are experts who can provide valuable insights, recommend strategies for financial sustainability, and help optimize your financial plan for self-sufficiency.

2.5 Securing the Right Location and Land

As you are preparing for all the essentials of no grid, you must pay attention to location. It means a lot if you want to live off the grid. Securing the right location and land is about choosing a place that aligns with your needs, goals, and the requirements of sustainable living.

In this chapter, you will explore all you need to know about securing the right location and land for your off-grid lifestyle. Check them out below.

- **Research Potential Areas:** Ensure you explore different regions, climates, and landscapes to find a location that suits your preferences and off-grid requirements. You should consider factors like local weather patterns, natural resources, land prices, and community demographics.

- **Define Your Criteria:** You need to understand what factors are important to you in a location. Also, you should consider aspects like climate, soil quality, water availability, sunlight exposure, zoning regulations, accessibility to essential services, and proximity to amenities.

- **Visit and Evaluate:** You must visit the potential locations in person to assess their suitability. Look for signs of natural beauty, biodiversity, and environmental resilience. Then, you evaluate the terrain, vegetation, water sources, and potential for sustainable food production.

- **Access to Resources:** Make sure the location provides access to essential resources for off-grid living, such as clean water sources (wells, rivers, and rainwater), sunlight for solar energy, arable land for gardening or farming, and materials for construction and infrastructure.

- **Long-Term Viability**: You should be futuristic while securing the right location. So, you have to think about the long-term viability of the location for off-grid living. Therefore, you need to consider factors like climate change projections, water availability trends, soil erosion risks, and evolving community dynamics that may impact your lifestyle sustainability.

- **Legal Considerations:** It is also important you understand the legal and regulatory landscape of the area, including zoning laws, building codes, land use restrictions, and permits required for off-grid installations (solar panels, water systems, etc.). Ensure you comply with local regulations to avoid future issues.

- **Community and Support:** You should take into consideration the local community and support networks available in the area. Off-grid living can be easier with like-minded neighbors, access to shared resources, and collaborative initiatives for sustainability and resilience.

- **Evaluate Risks:** Essentially, you need to assess potential risks and challenges associated with the location, such as natural disasters (floods, wildfires), environmental hazards, wildlife encounters, and seasonal variations in weather conditions. To stay safe, you must develop contingency plans and mitigation strategies.

2.6 Adapting to Different Environments and Climates

While preparing for no-grid living, you should bear in mind that you have to be adaptive. What you should understand, here, is adapting to different environments and climates is about being flexible, resourceful, and resilient no matter where you are. Now, let's discuss how you can approach adapting to different environments and climates in your off-grid journey.

- ❖ **Understand Climate Zones:** You should educate yourself about the climate zones in the areas you're considering for off-grid living. Different climates present unique challenges and opportunities, from extreme heat or cold to varying levels of precipitation.

❖ **Select Appropriate Technologies:** You can choose off-grid technologies and systems that are suitable for the specific climate and environment.

For example, in colder climates, you may need robust insulation, efficient heating systems, and strategies for snow management. In warmer climates, focus on cooling solutions, water conservation, and shade structures.

❖ **Water Management:** Ensure you adapt water management practices based on the local climate. In arid regions, you need to prioritize rainwater harvesting, water-efficient irrigation, and drought-resistant landscaping. In wetter climates, make sure you focus on drainage systems, flood prevention, and water storage capacity.

❖ **Energy Generation:** You should optimize your energy generation methods based on climate conditions. Solar panels work well in sunny regions, while wind turbines may be more effective in areas with consistent wind patterns. Consider hybrid systems or backup power options for unpredictable weather.

❖ **Food Production:** Make sure you design your food production strategies to suit the climate and growing seasons. Choose crops and gardening techniques that thrive in the local environment, such as cold-hardy vegetables for cooler climates or drought-resistant crops for arid regions. Also, you should use greenhouses or season extension methods for year-round production.

❖ **Building Design:** Design your off-grid structures to withstand climate-related challenges. I encourage you to use durable materials, proper insulation, and passive solar design principles for energy efficiency. You need to incorporate features like storm-resistant roofing, ventilation for hot climates, and snow load considerations for colder areas.

❖ **Fire Safety:** Be mindful of fire safety measures, especially in wildfire-prone regions. In addition, you should create defensible space around your property, use fire-resistant building materials, maintain clear access routes, and have a plan for evacuations or fire prevention strategies.

❖ **Community Engagement:** You must not underestimate the significance of community engagement in off-the-grid living. Trust me, you will learn a great deal about your local community experiences in adapting to the environment and climate. So, you have to make sure you collaborate on sustainable practices, share resources, and support each other during weather-related challenges or emergencies.

2.7 Legal and Regulatory Considerations

Addressing legal and regulatory considerations proactively can help you minimize legal risks, avoid potential conflicts, and enjoy a legally compliant and hassle-free off-grid lifestyle. It's crucial to understand and comply with laws, permits, and regulations to ensure a smooth and lawful off-grid experience. To stay safe, here's how you can approach legal and regulatory considerations in your off-grid journey:

- **Research Local Laws:** I will encourage you to start by researching the laws and regulations related to off-grid living in your chosen location. This includes zoning laws, building codes, land use regulations, environmental protections, and permits required for off-grid installations.

- **Consult Authorities:** The next thing you want to do is reach out to local authorities, such as planning departments, building inspectors, or environmental agencies, to clarify legal requirements and obtain accurate information. You should seek guidance on what permits or approvals are necessary for your off-grid systems and structures.

- **Compliance:** Ensure that your off-grid setup complies with all applicable laws and regulations. This may involve obtaining permits for solar panels, water collection systems, alternative septic systems, or other off-grid installations. Also, you have to adhere to building codes and safety standards to avoid legal issues.

- **Water Rights:** You should understand water rights and usage regulations in your area, especially if you rely on wells, rainwater harvesting, or water diversion methods. Then, you have to comply with water conservation measures and obtain necessary permits for water-related activities.

- **Environmental Impact:** Consider the environmental impact of your off-grid lifestyle and activities. Also, you should adhere to environmental laws, conservation practices, and land stewardship principles to minimize negative impacts on ecosystems, wildlife, and natural resources.

- **Easements and Access:** You also need to clarify easements, access rights, and property boundaries to avoid disputes with neighboring landowners. Ensure legal access to essential services, transportation routes, and emergency services.

- **Off-Grid Restrictions**: Be aware of any restrictions or limitations on off-grid living imposed by homeowners' associations, covenants, or neighborhood regulations. And ensure that your off-grid practices align with community guidelines and restrictions.

- **Legal Documentation:** You must keep thorough records and documentation related to your off-grid installations, permits, inspections, and approvals. This includes contracts, warranties, maintenance records, and communication with authorities.

- **Professional Assistance:** Importantly, you should seek legal advice or consult with professionals familiar with off-grid living and local regulations. They can provide legal guidance, help navigate complex issues, and ensure compliance with all legal requirements.

Chapter 3: Off-the-Grid Shelter Project

In any situation, shelter is among the most essential aspects of life. Without it, you will be left vulnerable and unsafe. As explained in chapter two, living off the grid has a lot of benefits, such as empowering you to live an independent lifestyle, becoming your own master, helping you achieve a free life, and many more. Having understood all these benefits, let's look at some off-the-grid shelter projects you can try, how you can plan and design your off-grid home, choose the best shelter options, heating and cooling solutions, and many more important topics.

3.1 Planning and Designing Your Off-Grid Home

When it comes to off-the-grid shelter projects, selecting, designing, planning, and carefulness is highly important. Once you understand what an off-grid system is all about and have chosen the kind of off-grid you want to build, your next step is planning and designing the home. The essence of this planning and designing is to ensure that your home isn't only functional but sustainable. Let's look at these steps.

Site analysis

Before you start designing your off-grid house, it's important to conduct a thorough site analysis, which includes studying the topography, soil, climate, and available resources in your land. A properly executed analysis will assist you in choosing the best location and orientation of your home and using the best natural resources.

Design concept

After conducting a site analysis, your next step is developing a design concept that will satisfy your needs and the natural landscape. The areas the design concept should cover include the style and look of the house, then its size and layout.

Floor plan

A floor plan is a detailed drawing that highlights the room's layout, the size of each room, and how the rooms are connected.

Also, when planning and designing your off-grid home, it's essential to consider the size of your family, their needs, and the activities they usually engage in.

Building materials

When it comes to designing your shelter, it's also crucial to choose suitable building materials. Materials that are sustainable, durable, and energy efficient are the best you should go for. Also, if you are on a tight budget, consider using local materials to reduce the transportation cost and also support local retailers.

Energy system

Off-grid systems need energy systems that can generate and store electricity independently. Therefore, when planning and designing your off-grid home, you must consider the type of energy that best suits your needs. You must choose from energy systems such as solar panels, wind turbines, or hydropower.

Water system

Given how crucial clean water is, this is an essential point to consider when planning your off-grid home. You must design a water system that can collect, purify, and store enough water for your living. One example of a popular water system option for off-grid is the rainwater harvesting system.

Waste management

Waste disposal is an essential part of house cleaning chores. You should design a waste management system that can assist you in effectively getting rid of waste safely and sustainably. Some popular off-grid house options are composting toilets and grey-water recycling systems.

Tips for planning and designing off-grid homes

I have some crucial tips you can consider when planning and designing off-grid homes. A few of these tips include:

- **Ensure you keep it simple**

Ensure you keep everything simple and avoid complicated things and designs requiring high-level maintenance or skills. Remember the famous quote, "Less is more."

- **Use local materials**

Using local materials enables you to save costs and also empower the local economy, and reduce transportation costs.

- **Maximize natural light**

Natural light is free and abundant. So, use it to reduce energy needs and save on utility bills.

- **Optimize energy efficiency**

Ensure you design your off-grid home to be as less energy-consuming as possible. You can achieve this by using energy-efficient appliances, using natural ventilation, and making sure that your home is well-insulated.

- **Plan for future expansion**

Whether you are starting a family or you already have one, it's essential to plan your house in a way that you have adequate space for future expansion, especially when the needs arise.

3.2 Building or Choosing Suitable Shelter Options

There are many different kinds of off-grid living, from creating your lodge to downsizing to minimalism in a tiny house and everything in between!

There is an off-grid home that is ideal for the life you envision, regardless of your style. Let's look at some of these options in detail.

Off Grid Homestead

One common misconception about off-grid living is that it's all about growing and sustaining your resources, but this isn't always true. Although this is a popular option, it's generally called homesteading. Homesteading is a lifestyle that revolves around self-sustainable living. Many "homesteaders" grow their food, make their cleaning and other household products from scratch, and focus on creating an independent household.

Aside from growing your food and cleaning items, the homestead has its own power and sources its water and sewage. These off-grid homes take independence and self-sufficiency to the next level by producing nearly everything they consume.

Off Grid Cabin or Residential Home

An off-grid cabin or residential home is the ideal place to live for those who desire to live in a more distant location while yet enjoying many aspects of their former lifestyle. These homes are similar to those seen in typical cities and neighborhoods, except for the absence of grid and municipality connections.

Finding power, water, and sewer is necessary when building a house off the regular road. These homes can look for more environmentally friendly solutions, even though it presents a problem during the design and construction phase. Living off the grid allows people to enjoy modern conveniences without relying on the overburdened system. They can do this by using renewable resources for power, pumping their own water, and managing their trash with compost alternatives.

An off-grid residential home enables you to live practically anywhere, whether your dream is to build a home nestled in the mountains like Martin Johnson, relocate to a cottage on a secluded island like Peter Van Stralen, or live surrounded by trees like the Vanwives. You may have the comforts of home and the tranquility of being in the middle of nature without giving up the conveniences of living off the grid.

Tiny homes

When deciding to transition to an off-the-grid living system, many consider it an opportunity to downsize. They accomplish a sense of fulfillment by embracing a minimalist lifestyle and valuing experience over things. This helps sustainability, as the less you use, the less waste you will produce. While you can achieve these minimalistic options in a smaller version of residential homes, there are numerous creative options for downsizing off-grid.

Geodesic Dome

A Geodesic Dome was first introduced after World War I to be used as a planetarium. It was also revered for the magnitude of its enclosed surface and its weight-bearing abilities. "A geodesic dome is a hemispherical thin-shell structure (lattice-shell) based on a geodesic polyhedron. The triangular elements of the dome are structurally rigid and distribute the structural stress throughout the structure, making geodesic domes able to withstand hefty loads for their size."

Container Home

Another notable option for an off-grid house is a container home. A shipping container home is built using recycled containers as the home's structure. Their uniformity gives an excellent blank canvas to create a home with clean lines and modern architecture. Furthermore, container homes are increasingly getting recognition because they promote sustainability by recycling. Shipping containers are used daily to move items worldwide; therefore, by revitalizing old containers into modern ones, you are reducing waste.

Earthships

As more people are shifting to the off-grid home system, the desire to live sustainably also increases. People are constantly evaluating their lifestyles and searching for more ways to reduce waste. A vital upgrade that has aided this movement is a resurgence of Earthship utilization.

"Earthships are designed to behave as passive solar earth shelters made of natural and upcycled materials such as earth-packed tires. Earthships may feature a variety of amenities and aesthetics and are designed to withstand the extreme temperatures of a desert, staying close to 70 °F (21 °C) regardless of outside weather conditions."

They focus on repurposing recycled materials and can operate with minimal reliance on public electricity and fossil fuels. Earthships are among the best off-grid home choices, especially with how Earthship Biotecture and Earthship Overland share mind-boggling, off-grid Earthship masterpieces.

3.3 Energy-Efficient and Sustainable Design Techniques

Wondering how you can reduce energy consumption in your home? Here are some energy-efficient and sustainable design techniques you can adopt.

Begin with a smart design

Creating energy-efficient homes starts with an intelligent design. You should be familiar with all the necessary steps to building a home so that the builders and constructors can implement these strategies cost-effectively; parameters you should ask your designers or constructors to pay attention to. Ensure tailed communication between you and the workers to avoid crucial details falling through the cracks.

Use the Sun for Solar Tempering

Using the sun for heating through south-facing windows during winter reduces heating costs. Shade the windows in summer to reduce cooling costs. Solar tempering allows for optimizing the passive use of the sun's heat without spending on thermal mass. You should address solar tempering during the design phase.

Optimize with Energy Modeling

A home's energy is estimated during the design phase using energy modeling software to ensure that your home achieves net zero energy while reducing costs. Based on the result, you can use or modify everything to balance building performance and construction costs.

Super-Seal the Building Envelope

Super-sealing building envelopes is the most effective solution builders can take to improve the energy efficiency of a zero net energy home.

There are many proven air sealing strategies available, so select an approach that perfectly blends with your climate, skills, and budget.

Super-Insulate the Building Envelope

After making your home airtight, super-insulating the house is the second most cost-effective strategy for creating a zero-energy house. Energy modeling, as mentioned above, can help you optimize the insulation levels for the ceiling, walls, and floors. Select framing strategies that make it easier to insulate the building envelope and minimize thermal bridging.

Create an Energy Efficient, Fresh Air Supply

Generally, zero-energy homes are airtight. Therefore, it's essential to create a continuous source of fresh air. You can opt for appliances like heat recovery ventilation (HRV) systems or energy recovery ventilation (ERV) systems that expel stale air while recovering its heat and returning it to the home with fresh air.

Choose an energy-efficient heating and cooling system

Highly efficient, cost-effective heating and cooling systems are essential to meeting the net zero energy goal. Among the perfect choices are air-source ductless heat pumps, also called mini-split heat pumps.

The systems are energy efficient and lack the cons of central, forced-air systems or the high costs of thermal heat pumps.

Install Energy Efficient Lighting

LED lights are the perfect solution for achieving zero-net net energy homes. They are more energy efficient than CFLs, durable, and contain zero mercury. Additionally, they can meet different lighting needs, including bright white light and soft, warm light.

Use the Sun for Renewable Energy

Grid-tied solar photovoltaic (PV) panels nowadays provide the most cost-effective form of renewable energy. They can power all a home's energy needs, including lighting, heating and cooling systems, appliances, and hot water. However, they are the most expensive component of a zero-energy home, and strategies for reducing or mitigating those costs are important to consider.

3.4 DIY Off-the-Grid Shelter Projects (Building Your Shelter)

Whether you want to transform your current house off the grid or build from scratch in nature, desert, or snow, here are some simple ways to create an off-the-grid shelter.

Turn Your Home Into a Shelter

Over the last few decades, more and more householders have transitioned to off-grid home systems upon realizing the impact on the environment and understanding the importance of reducing their footprint. Most decided to go green or off-grid to increase their house value and save on utility bills. Here are steps to follow to turn your home off-grid.

- **Solar installation**

The first and most straightforward way to transition to living green is to install solar panels in your house and eliminate the utility power supply. You can ask experts for the number of solar panels that will be sufficient for your home and deliver an adequate amount of light. However, keep in mind that this approach can be inefficient and highly expensive unless you live in a home that was built 3-5 years ago. Most houses built longer than these years are generally never designed to be taken off the grid. Many of your household appliances were probably fixed on energy, making it far beyond just changing to LED lights. But, if you are ready to take these steps, there are many energy-efficient appliances you can replace those power-consuming ones, and this has brought us to the next step:

- **The smart way to go off-grid**

This method involves a lot of work and planning, but if effectively executed, it will save you time and cost. Moreover, you are changing your home system to be more energy efficient instead of just stuffing your home with new appliances. First, you must look at the larger energy consumer in your home, the water heater. Here, you have many options for making your water heater energy efficient, which include placing a blanket on its top to insulate it further and prevent heat from escaping, reducing the thermostat temperature as the higher the temperature difference between the water in the heater and the ambient air, the higher the losses. Or add a timer; Timers are quite debated as you have to follow a strict routine to see any savings and to avoid having the occasional cold shower. Basically, you want the timer to only switch the heater on once a day. An hour later, the heater should be turned off, and everyone should shower. The water should then remain cold until the next day when the timer turns on again. If you can't follow this type of routine, a timer will probably not have much effect on your electrical bill. Another option is to change your water heater to a solar one.

This type of heater sits in a sunny spot on the roof and uses black vacuum tubes to harness the heat from the sun and use it to heat your water and keep it warm. The heater usually has an element to boost the water temperature when there is no sun throughout the day.

Kitchen Appliances

Oven and stove
Unless you cook a lot, the cooker and oven won't significantly impact your long-term energy savings. However, changing them will significantly lower your evening peak demand, contributing to lesser inverter usage and, to a lesser extent, a larger battery bank capacity. The best solution to an off-the-grid home is gas stoves and gas ovens.

Refrigerator
This only applies to refrigerators that are more than ten years old. Modern refrigerators feature new digital inverter-based refrigeration systems and much better insulation that allow them to function on lower electricity and longer cooling times. Your solar installation will be smaller as a result of these long-term savings.

Build a Shelter in Nature

Several methods of building shelter are available, including:
Creating an A-frame shelter
This shelter will keep you warm and prevent colds from getting in. To start:
- Lean a big, long branch towards a tree to build the frame.
- Lean smaller sticks against that branch close together.
- Ensure the ends of the sticks on the sides don't stick out too far at the top, or they will catch the rain, and it will be dripping inside your shelter.
- Add spruce branches or moss on top of the sticks.
- At last, you add leaves or other debris to seal it all off.

The lean-to
This shelter is a good choice if you want one that you can sit down inside to begin:
- First, you need to find two sticks with a branch growing on them to build the frame.
- Cut or break off the stick about 10 cm from where the branch grows, and cut off the branch 10 cm from the stick as well.
- Hammer both sticks into the ground and fit a long, solid branch on top of them.
- Lean some sticks against that one and weave smaller twigs into them diagonally.
- Attach spruce branches onto the twigs from the bottom up.
The lean-to with a raised bed

This is a great shelter in cold weather to build
- Look for two trees, each with a branch growing on them.
- Start by building the bed. Place some straight sticks diagonally on a couple of logs on the ground on each side. This will make your bed a little springy too.
- Add small spruce twigs or dry grass as bedding for extra comfort and insulation.
- For the roof, find a long branch to rest on the branches of the two trees.
- Lean many sticks against the top. and then weave smaller twigs into them diagonally.
- Make sure the roof is steep.
- At last, you weave spruce branches onto the twigs from the bottom up.

Build a Shelter in the Desert

Below-ground desert shelter
- Find a low spot or depression between dunes or rocks. If necessary, dig a trench 45 to 60 centimeters (18 to 24 inches) deep and long and wide enough for you to lie in comfortably.
- Pile the sand from the trench to form a mound around three sides.
- On the open end of the trench, dig out more sand so you can get in and out of your shelter easily.
- Cover the trench with your material.
- Secure the material in place using sand, rocks, or other weights.

Snow Shelter

Snow cave
This shelter is best for sloped ground, deep snow, and hunkering down during a storm. Mark your shelter above the surface with branches or ski poles so passersby don't walk or ski on the roof. Always poke at least one ventilation hole in the ceiling. During a snowstorm, periodically clear vents to maintain airflow.

- Look for snow at least 6 feet deep (measure with a probe if unsure). Snowbanks and wind-drifted snow work great.
- Shape the ceiling into a dome for greater strength, and smooth it out to prevent dripping.
- Dig the entrance of your shelter downhill off and below your sleeping shelf for maximum warmth (heat rises) and ease of snow removal.

3.5 Heating and Cooling Solutions Without Reliance On the Grid

Many homeowners find it appealing to realize they can use heating and cooling systems that don't rely on electric or gas companies. There are numerous options if you want to opt for an off-grid heating and cooling system.

- **Solar energy:** solar energy enables you to utilize the sun to cool or heat water in your home.
- **Geothermal heating and cooling:** This heating and cooling system uses the earth's constant temperature to heat and cool your home. A geothermal heat pump is installed underground, and a series of pipes circulate a water and antifreeze mixture to transfer heat to and from the earth.
- **Wood-burning stove:** A wood-burning stove can be used to heat your home and can also be used to cook food.
- **Passive solar design:** This method involves using the sun's energy directly; some popular options include using South-facing windows to allow sunlight to enter and mass material to absorb and store heat.

3.6 Building and Using Composting Toilets

A composting toilet is a system that gathers and composts human waste, enabling you to turn the useless residue into a valuable resource to use in your lawn or garden. Although it resembles the traditional composting system, the modern method is made healthier, sustainable, and more environmentally friendly.

Materials needed
- Pocket hole jig
- Electric drill
- Drill bits
- Jigsaw
- Screwdriver
- Woodworking file
- Sandpaper

Procedure
- First, measure everything, including the toilet seats, desired height, and all the necessary measurements. Then, cut the plywood for the top and four planks of wood to make the four sides of the box.
- Cut a hole in the center of the plywood piece.
- Paint or stain the box.
- Add the urine separator.
- Attach the toilet seats using screws.
- Build a leg for the wooden box.
- Place the bucket inside the structure.

Chapter 4: Off-the-Grid Power Solutions

The increase in pollution is continuously affecting soil quality every day in both urban and rural areas; this is one of the reasons many people are adopting off-grid power solutions that enable them to reduce their footprint and become more green. In this chapter, we will explore some superb off-grid power solutions such as solar energy, wind and hydropower options, micro-hydro systems, energy storage and management, and many more.

4.1 Solar Energy

Solar power is energy from the sun that is converted into thermal or electrical energy. It is the cleanest and most abundant renewable energy source available.

Harnessing Solar Power

Solar is the best alternative energy source, this makes it necessary to know the various ways to harness solar power. You can utilize solar energy in three ways: PV cells transform energy from the sun into electricity through solar panels. In the case of solar thermal energy, the energy trapped in hot water or steam is stored and used to generate clean and sustainable electricity. The third method to harness solar energy is by using and replacing daily life products with solar-installed ones. In recent years, photovoltaic cell costs have dropped considerably, making it easy to use solar panels even in average homes. More people are coming forward to invest in solar power projects, with even more commercial businesses offering support to it. Several products are customized these days to fit into solar technology for functionality.

Understanding and Designing Your Solar System

Solar photovoltaic or solar power system is a renewable energy system that uses PV modules to convert sunlight into electricity. The generated electricity can be stored or used directly, fed back into the grid line, or combined with other electricity generators or renewable energy sources.

Solar PV system is a very reliable and clean source of electricity that can suit a wide range of applications such as residence, industry, agriculture, livestock, etc. Designing your solar system is a process that actually requires meticulous planning and a comprehensive understanding of various components and factors. A well-designed system ensures efficiency, safety, and cost-effectiveness.

- **Figure out how much power you need**

Planning to insert a solar system without understanding how much power you need is like traveling without knowing your destination. Use a kWh calculator to add everything you'll power with your solar power system.

- **Calculate the amount of battery storage you need.**

Since you have figured out how much power your home needs, it's time to determine how many batteries you need to store. Consider your local weather trends. How often do you have several days with little or no sunlight in a row? When the output of your solar panels is significantly less than what they can produce, your batteries must be able to hold you over. Do you require enough batteries to last for three or four days or longer, or just enough for a day or two of storage? Do you possess an additional power source that you may use in an emergency, such as a generator or turbine? Do you plan to store the batteries in a cold place or an insulated room? Answering these questions will allow you to choose the best battery storage. The recommended storage temperature for batteries is 77°F, or 25°C. They are less effective in colder rooms, so you'll need a larger battery bank—more than 50% larger in below-freezing temperatures! Each of these responses impacts the battery bank's size and, consequently, its price. Which battery bank voltage 12, 24, or 48 volts should you use? Higher voltage battery banks are typically associated with larger systems. This minimizes the number of parallel strings and lowers the current flowing between the battery bank and the inverter. A 12V battery bank makes sense if you plan a small system and want to run your RV's 12V DC appliances and charge your phone. However, you should think about 24-volt and 48-volt systems if you need to power considerably more than 2000 Watts at once. It will also enable you to employ thinner and less costly copper cables between the batteries and the inverter and lower the number of parallel strings of batteries you'll need. For the majority of permanently off-grid households, a 48V system works well.

- **Calculate the number of solar panels needed for your location and time of year**

Once you discover the energy you need to make daily, you must understand how much sunlight you require. This energy from the sun for a given location is called "sun hours." The number of sun hours at a location is not the number of daylight hours.

It is how many hours 1000 Watts worth of solar radiation strikes a square meter of surface area at the location over a day. The sun isn't as bright at 8 AM as it is at noon, so an hour of morning sun may be counted as half an hour, whereas the hour from noon to 1 PM would be complete.

Unless you live near the equator, you do not have the same number of hours of sunlight in the winter as you do in the summer. When designing an off-grid solar system – especially one that will be counted on to provide your electricity day in and day out, be conservative.

Take the worst-case scenario of sun hours for your area by using the season with the least sunshine during the period you'll be using the system (i.e., winter if your system will be powering a full-time residence). This way, you won't fall short on solar energy for part of the year. If your system is used for a summer camp or seasonal vacation cabin, you don't need to plan for winter, but if it is a year-round home or a hunting cabin, you need to use the number of sun hours corresponding to winter.

- **Choose a solar charge controller**

Now that you have your batteries and solar, you need a way to put the power from the solar into the batteries. A rough calculation to know the size of the solar charge controller you need is to take the Watts from the solar and divide it by the battery bank voltage. Add another 25% for a safety factor.

However, choosing a charge controller involves some additional considerations. PWM and MPPT are the two main types of technologies available for charge controllers. To put it briefly, you can utilize a PWM charge controller if the voltage of the battery bank and the solar panel array match. Therefore, you can use a PWM using a 12V panel and a 12V battery bank. An MPPT charge controller is required if the voltage of your solar panel and battery bank differ and cannot be connected in series to make them match. An MPPT charge controller is required if you have a 12V battery bank and a 20V solar panel. A 48V battery bank and an MPPT charge controller are your best options for building a whole-home system.

- **Select an inverter**

If you are running only DC loads, then you can skip this step, but if you run AC, which you probably do, then you are required to convert the direct current from the batteries into alternating current for your appliances. You must know the type of AC power you need. Check the output voltage specs of the inverter you are interested in carefully to ensure it matches your needs.

Installation and Maintenance

Installation
The first step in solar installation is checking for roof conditions. If your roof is old or damaged, the installation might not last long. Next is to ensure your roof slope is between 10 and 30 degrees to allow for appropriate rainfall drainage and debris removal. Get experts to analyze how much weight your roof can sustain. Next, assess your building energy to know the number of needed panels.

Maintenance
Maintaining your solar by removing dirt and debris can enhance its life and durability. Let's look at the steps to clean and maintain your solar.

- Schedule regular cleaning: At least one at the end of winter and one after fall.
- Choose the right maintenance time, which should be early morning when the panels are fresh. Cleaning them when they are still warm or exposed to direct sunlight may be counterproductive, as combining heat and cold water can generate thermal stresses and damage the equipment. Avoid when windy, rainy, or snowy.
- Clean gently
- Carry out a visual inspection to check for damages like cracks, breaks, or loose connections
- Allow the panels to air dry, or use clean clothes to wipe them.

Solar Batteries

Whether you are a new homeowner or want to change your home to be all-green, in this subchapter, you will get answers to all your questions about selecting solar batteries.

Solar batteries store the energy your panels generate when you need it. There are four main types of batteries used in the solar world.

- **Lead-Acid**

These batteries have low energy capacity, but they remain the most cost-effective solar batteries available. Lead-acid batteries come in both flooded and sealed varieties. They can be classified as either shallow cycles or deep cycles depending on the intended function and safe depth of discharge (DOD).

- **Lithium-Ion**

They have higher energy density than lead-acid. It allows you to access more energy stored within the battery before recharging. The only disadvantage of this battery is that it's expensive and can potentially catch fire due to an effect known as thermal runaway.

- **Nickel-cadmium**

These batteries are rarely used in residential settings but rather in airlines and industries due to their high durability and ability to function in extreme temperatures.
Unfortunately, cadmium is a dangerous element that, when disposed of inappropriately, can hurt the environment.

- **Flow**

Flow batteries offer high efficiency, with a depth of discharge of 100%, but they have a low energy density. They are costly due to their size, which makes them costly and impractical for households.

4.2 Wind and Hydro Power Options

If you don't wish to go for solar power as an option, then you can rest assured and check for the wind and hydropower options, which we will discuss in detail in this subchapter.

Understanding Wind Turbines

The principle by which wind turbines work is quite simple: rather than using electricity to make wind like a fan does, wind turbines do the opposite by using wind to make electricity. The wind turns the propeller-like blades of a turbine around a rotor, which spins a generator, which creates electricity.

Wind is formed by the combination of the sun unevenly heating the atmosphere, irregularities of the earth's surface, and the earth's rotation. A wind turbine turns wind energy into electricity using the aerodynamic force from the rotor blades, which work like an airplane wing or helicopter rotor blade. After the wind blows, the air pressure on one side of the blade reduces. The air pressure difference between the two blades creates lift and drag. The lift's force is greater than the drag, which causes the rotor to spin. The rotor connects to the generator, either directly or through a shaft and a series of gears that speed up the rotation and allow for a physically smaller generator. This translation of aerodynamic force to the rotation of a generator creates electricity.

Choosing the Right Wind Turbine

The majority of wind turbines are categorized into two:

- **Horizontal-Axis Turbines**

They commonly have three blades and operate upwind with the turbine pivoting at the top of the tower so the blades face into the wind.

- **Vertical axis turbines**

They usually come in different varieties, such as the eggbeater-style Darrieus model, named after its French inventor. You don't need to adjust these turbines to point into the wind for them to work.

Installation and Maintenance

Installing wind turbines requires careful planning and design. To achieve this first,

- Prepare your land by conducting environmental impact studies, identifying suitable areas, and building roads and platforms to transport the installation components.
- Construct the base using reinforced concrete.
- Transport the turbine components.
- Next is to assemble the items. Assemble the tower sections, install the nacelle, and mount the blades on the rotor shaft.
- The last step is to assemble the wind turbines and connect them to the electrical network.

Maintenance

Once you install the wind turbines, it's essential to carry out maintenance to ensure efficiency and enhance its durability. Maintenance should include inspection and replacement of worn components, cleaning of blades, and updating control and safety systems.

Hydropower Options

Hydropower usually obtains its energy from streams or rivers. It works by channeling some water from the river along a different path. The diverted water turns a turbine. This turbine powers a generator, which produces electricity. Hydropower options save money. It's reliable, green energy, and an off-grid solution. There are two main types of hydropower turbines: reaction and impulse. The type of hydropower turbine selected for a project is based on the height of standing water, referred to as "head," and the flow, or volume of water over time, at the site.

4.3 Micro-Hydro System to Generate Electricity

One of the most accessible and most reliable renewable energy sources for your home may be micro-hydropower. You can think about installing a hydropower system on your land if water is running through it to produce electricity. Typically, micro-hydropower plants may produce up to 100 kW of electricity. Microhydropower systems include most hydropower systems utilized by small company owners and homeowners, including farmers and ranchers. Nonetheless, a 10-kilowatt micro hydropower system can often supply sufficient electricity for a sizable house, a modest resort, or a hobby farm.

To turn the energy of flowing water into energy, which is then transformed into electricity, a micro hydropower system requires a turbine, pump, or waterwheel. The micro hydro system consists of three components: the water conveyance, a channel that delivers water, a turbine, pump, or waterwheel that transforms the energy of flowing water into rotational energy. An alternator or generator transforms the rotational energy into electricity, and a regulator controls the generator. Then, wiring that delivers the electricity.

4.4 Energy Storage, Management, and Conservation

Energy can be stored in different ways, including

- Pumped hydroelectric: Water is pumped up to a reservoir via the use of electricity. Water released from the reservoir turns a turbine to produce energy.
- Compressed air: Air is compressed by electricity at a rate of up to 1,000 pounds per square inch and stored, frequently in caverns beneath the surface. An expansion turbine generator uses the pressured air to provide energy during periods of high demand.
- Flywheels: A flywheel, a rotor, is accelerated by electricity, allowing the energy to be preserved as kinetic rotational energy. The flywheel's rotating force powers a generator when energy is required. Certain flywheels use magnetic bearings, run in a vacuum to reduce drag, and have spinning speeds of up to 60,000 rpm.
- AA batteries: Very large batteries have the same capacity as regular rechargeable batteries in that they can hold electricity until needed. Lithium-ion, lead acid, lithium-ion, and other battery technologies can be used in these systems.
- Thermal reserve of energy: Thermal energy can be produced using electricity and stored for later use. For instance, in periods of low demand, power can be utilized to make chilled water or ice, which can then be used for cooling during periods of peak electricity usage.

4.5 Backup Power Systems

Gone were those days when your only option was the fuel-powered standby generators. Some of the popular backup power systems available today include:

- **Home Battery**

Home battery backup system usually stores energy, which can be used for powerhouses during an outage. The batteries usually obtain their power from your solar system.

- **Generators**

You can install a generator on natural gas connected to your home. This means you don't have to manually refill them.

Chapter 5: Water Management

A water management system ensures that water is efficiently used and distributed in your home. This system is essential in conserving water and reducing waste and pollution. In this chapter, you will learn how to understand water management systems, including source and treat water, techniques for rainwater harvesting, DIY water filtration systems, purification of off-grid hot water, and many more.

5.1 Sourcing and Treating Water

Water sourcing and treatment is about obtaining the cleanest water for domestic and commercial use. Generally, water treatment depends on the source of the water. For instance, if the water is from the surface, such as a lake or river, then the problem you might need to treat is particulate matter. But if the water comes from the ground through mountain springs, then the water quality is good, which means you only need to disinfect it. One of the biggest problems of water around the globe is that today, most drinking water sources are exposed to pollution and require appropriate treatment to eliminate the disease-causing elements. The standard method to treat water include:

- **Coagulation and flocculation**

These are mostly the first stages of water treatment. Here, you will add positively charged elements; the positive charge will neutralize the negative charge of dirt and other dissolved particles in the water. After this, the particles attach to the chemicals, creating larger clumps.

- **Sedimentation wastewater treatment**

During sedimentation, the mass settles to the bottom of the water supply due to its weight. Sedimentation is the process of depositing the masses and dirt to the bottom, and it can be used in groundwater treatment methods.

- **Purification**

The filtration process is a type of water treatment. Once the mass settles at the bottom of the water supply, the clear water at the top will pass through filters of different compositions (sand, gravel, or charcoal) and different pore sizes to remove dissolved particles, such as dust, parasites, bacteria, viruses, and other substances.

- **Cleansing**

Once you filter the water, the next step is to add disinfectants like chlorine and chloramine, which will kill any remaining harmful particles inside the water.

5.2 Techniques for Rainwater Harvesting and Groundwater Sourcing

Rainwater harvesting is a simple and easy method to harvest and store rainwater for future uses. This process requires collecting and storing water using artificially designed systems that run off natural or artificial catchment areas, e.g., rooftops, compounds, rocky surfaces, hill slopes, or artificially repaired impervious/semi-pervious land surfaces. You can filter the collected rainwater use or store it. Rainwater harvesting has many advantages, such as reducing water bills, offering ecological benefits, reducing erosion and flooding around buildings, providing adequate means for Irrigation purposes, and reducing demand for groundwater.

There are two primary techniques for rainwater harvesting and groundwater sourcing:

Surface rainwater sourcing

This involves the flowing of rainwater as surface runoff which you can store and use later. To store this water, divert the flow of small creeks and streams into your reservoir or underground. You can use the water for farming, cattle or for domestic purposes. This method is best used in urban areas.

You can harvest rooftop rainwater/storm runoff in urban places through:
- Recharge Pit
- Recharge Trench
- Tubewell
- Recharge Well

Groundwater

Groundwater recharge is the downward movement of water from surface to groundwater and it's a hydrologic process. The main method through which the water enters an aquifer is recharge. By using artificial recharge techniques, the surplus will then recharge the groundwater aquifers.

You can harvest rainwater in rural areas through:
- Gully Plug
- Contour Bund
- Dugwell Recharge
- Percolation Tank
- Check Dam/Cement Plug/Nala Bund
- Recharge Shaft

Rooftop water usually flows as runoff. Since it's fresh, you can store it for future purposes. If you want to store surface water, divert the flow of small creeks and streams into reservoirs on the surface or underground. The water can be utilized for farming or any domestic use. This method of water harvesting is mostly used in urban sites.

5.3 DIY Water Filtration System and Purification

The best way to ensure you drink the healthiest water is by filtering it. Although you can purchase bottled water that is already filtered, you can take charge of getting your own clean water by filtering it yourself. This way, you will save costs and enjoy healthier living. Whichever method you choose to purify your water will depend on your efforts, budget, and water quality. To filter your water at home, you can choose to obtain a small home filter, alternatively, you can follow any of these methods.

- **Boiling**

Heating water for relatively one minute makes it safe to drink. After you heat it, you can transfer it to a medium where it will cool down. The boiling will kill most of the harmful organisms inside the water. But this is not always the safest way because some bacteria cannot be killed by heat, thus you can opt for disinfects.

- **Use tablets and drops**

Some available disinfectant tablets for purifying water are sodium, dichloro isocyanurate, chlorine dioxide iodine, and tetraglycine hydroperiodide. To use any of them, follow the manufacturer's instructions written in the package.

- **UV treatment**

In this approach, you allow ultraviolet sunlight to shine through the water. This damages the DNA of harmful germs, disinfecting the water by removing bacteria, viruses, and other microorganisms. Adding lime juice can help speed up the solar treatment process

- **Activated charcoal**

Activated charcoal can take up and store toxic compounds, smells, and germs. It can also reduce fluoride and heavy metals. But it's ineffective at removing bacteria, viruses, or hard water minerals.

- **Travel-size sediment filters**

These are store-bought filters designed to eliminate germs and bacteria from water. They usually come in different forms, like a hand pump machine, a filtering straw or water bottle, squeezable pouch filters, and a water pitcher.

DIY portable sediment filters
You can create your own water filter to remove smell and debris by layering a mix of gravel, play sand, and activated carbon in a bucket drilled with a hole and fit with plumbing to pour water through.

- **Fruit peel filters**

Sometimes, people use fruit peelers to purify water in villages that rely on contaminated water for survival. You can adopt this method into your DIY filtration system.

5.4 Water Pump with Solar Panels

Essentially, solar-powered convert the sun's rays (photons) to electricity that will operate the water pump. It uses solar panels to collect the photons (units of light) from sunlight, producing the direct current (DC) that provides the energy for the motor to pump water out from its source. An inverter is used if the pump motor needs alternating current (AC) rather than DC.

The components of the solar water pump include:
- Solar panels that take the sun's photons and convert them to electricity.

- A water pump motor that takes water from any available water source, like underground, can be used for household chores.
- Inverter: Water pumps run on AC electrical current, so the inverter converts the electricity from the original DC to usable AC.
- Pipes: Pipes will transport water from the original source to wherever it needs to go: a purification system, a holding tank, etc.
- Water tank: The water pumping system often includes a tank to store water that may be used when sunshine isn't available.
- Pump controllers: The controllers regulate the water pump and allow it to be turned on and off. They can increase the life of the water pump by protecting it from electrical irregularities or motor damage if it keeps running when a water source runs dry. Controllers also maximize water delivery.

Overall, solar-powered water has benefits, including the fact that it's economical to operate, it's eco-friendly, useful in many areas, easy to maintain, reliable, easy to install, and helps increase productivity.

5.5 Water Conservation and Storage Solutions

Life sometimes happens unexpectedly. So, we need to understand how to store water at home and be ready for everything that comes our way. Though it sounds horrifying and unsettling, anyone can find themselves without access to water. Storing water for unanticipated emergencies is the only way to deal with this. Earthquakes, hurricanes, and tornadoes are natural calamities that can damage or contaminate our water supply systems. Let's look at some means of storing water for given durations.

Storing Water for a Month or Longer

- **Cistern or tanks**

This medium is most suitable if you want to store water for longer periods. They are made of sturdy, food-grade plastic or concrete and are enormous. You can also use them to collect rainwater. The only disadvantage of cisterns or tanks is that they tend to take up space. Unless your home has abundant space, it's best to check for other methods.

- **Water Barrels**

Barrels, aside from giving you a 55-gallon storage capacity, are made of food-grade plastic and perfect for heavy-duty use. They are blue, which means they will stop algae growth by limiting light, and lastly, the plastic is UV-resistant and BPA-free. This is why barrels are the first choice for many people when storing water.

- **WaterBOB Bathtub Water Storage Container**

WaterBOBs can hold up to a hundred gallons of water. You can place them in your bathtub and fill them with water from your faucet. They are extremely sanitary and protect the water from any contamination. The only problem here is that these plastic containers are not exactly emergency-friendly. You must store water in advance, which may not be possible in sudden calamities.

Storing Water for a Fortnight or So

- **Regular water bottles**

If you have purified your water and believe it is healthy enough for instant uptake, you can purchase regular water bottles from any convenience store, fill them with water, and store them.

- **2. 5-gallon Water Jugs**

These jugs are heavy-duty and blue. The reason for its coloration, as mentioned earlier, is to restrict light and eliminate algae formation. Once you purchase them, carefully wash them, allow them to dry, and sanitize them with bleach to ensure they are completely safe for use.

5.6 Off-Grid Hot Water

There are so many ways to heat water naturally on your homestead. In this subchapter, you will explore some of these methods, which, at the end of your reading, will make you feel confident that building an off-grid water heater is easy and pretty cheap.

- **Off-grid Propane Hot Water Heater**

While propane technically is not an off-the-grid element because you have to rely on another entity to provide energy, it's an effective method that most greeners use to obtain hot water. Even though the increase in demand for propane tankless water heaters has made it expensive recently, it's still among the cheapest methods of getting hot water for off-the-grid enthusiasts.

- **Solar Hot Water Heater Systems**

Another method to heat your water effectively and freely is using the sun's power. I believe you have experienced how hot water comes from a medium that sat in the sun for a long time. To achieve a maximum result, ensure the medium is black, as a black surface is a good conductor of heat.

- **Off the Grid Wood-Burning Hot Water Heater**

A wood-burning water heater is an excellent choice for those living off-grid as it provides a reliable source of hot water without relying on electricity or other fuel sources.

It is a self-sufficient and sustainable option that allows you to utilize readily available resources such as fallen trees or branches. Additionally, wood is a renewable fuel source that is often cheaper and more accessible than other heating options. Unfortunately, there are some downsides to using this method, like the fact that it's time-consuming and requires many efforts.

- **Electric Water Heating Systems for Off Grid Living**

Improving electric tankless water heaters is a crucial development advantageous to greeners. Not only do these new electric tankless heaters use less power, but they also provide a steady flow of hot water, so you don't have to worry about running out in the middle of a shower. And because they don't have a tank, they take up less space, making them an excellent option for those with limited room. Also, with no tank to worry about, you'll never have to deal with the hassle of replacing a leaky or rusty tank.

Chapter 6: Off-the-Grid Food Production and Preservation

Before the invention of the refrigerator and other modern food preservation methods, older generations had many ways to produce and preserve their food, which we will discuss in detail in this chapter alongside other important subtopics like ways you can grow your food, raise livestock, and poultry, embrace permaculture principles, practical food storage and food storage containers, emergency food storage, advanced food storage methods and many more. Without further delay, let's check out what this chapter has for you.

6.1 Sustainable Food Production

Have you ever thought about how the food you eat is produced? You will be surprised to hear that your food might be unsustainable. This makes it more important to change our lifestyle to become more sustainable, especially with increased food insecurity and climate change. Sustainable food production is a method of producing food without damaging the environment. It ensures that the food is economically efficient and can be ideally used in the future. Establishing more sustainable food production methods will protect the planet and provide better access to food for people around the globe. Sustainability has always been crucial, and lack of it can lead to many consequences including it causes environmental degradation, climate change, and food and water insecurity. There are many ways you can venture into sustainable food production and be part of those changing the world for the better.

Growing Your Food

Growing your food, like crops, vegetables, and fruits, is one of the most rewarding experiences you will ever have. Well, we can say — "You are enjoying the fruit of your labor." The benefits of growing your food are plenty.

First, tending to your plants is relaxing, especially for greeners; you feel closer to your food as you dirty your hands with soil, you are honing new therapeutic skills, and you get your vitamin D refilled all the time. Let's not forget the fresh produce you will always bring home.

And before you realize it, your home will be screaming with fresh and healthy food. So, how can you grow your food? Here are a few steps:

- **Find the Perfect Spot**

Just like how everything in your home needs to be kept in the perfect spot, the first step of growing your food is finding the right spot for it. Take time to examine your garden and understand where you can grow certain crops.

- **Sunshine**

Plants love the sun; at least they need about six to eight hours of sunlight daily. This means you must avoid constantly shaded spots, although some plants thrive well in shade. For instance, leafy greens such as Swiss Chard and salad leaves thrive best under shade or amidst taller trees. But overall, the best thing to do is to look for sunny areas.

- **Access to water**

Your plants need to be watered regularly, and ensure your space has a constant supply of water to keep them healthy, moist, and hydrated.

- **Choose the right soil**

The suitable soil completes the trifecta for your garden's necessities. Look for soil that is rich in organic nutrients.

- **Decide what you want to grow**

Now that you have prepared the space for your plants, enjoy the fun of deciding what you want to grow. Think strategically; for instance, if you are in a rural space where your neighborhood grows corn and cauliflower, you can remove these two from your list. If you want easy and fast results, consider growing items like arugula, lettuce, and baby spinach. Baby carrots and tomatoes are also among easy to grow crops.

- **Start Planting**

Keep in mind that regardless of what you plant, you have two options to choose from. You can purchase already-grown shrubs and plant them in your space or use seeds, this means you will start the planting from scratch. For seeds, you begin growing them indoors in winter time then move them outside when the weather starts getting warm.

Here are some notes to remember when planting:

- **Avoid Stressing or Overheating your Plants When Moving Them.**
  Try to separate the plant's roots if they are densely packed so they can stretch out and grow further in the soil. Transplant your plants very deep under the soil.

- **Keep Them Watered and Supported**

Once your plants are planted, water them instantly to help them settle. After that, you should continue to water them at least one inch of water weekly. You can even understand when your plants need water when they wilt. Some plants produce their seeds underground, while others grow in height.

- **It's Time for Harvest**

Within a few weeks or months after planting, your grows might be ready for harvest. Most times, you will know when your crops have ripped. Plants like tomatoes and peppers will change color, while others like carrots can be harvested in big sizes and small.

Raising Livestock and Poultry

There are many things you need to note when it comes to raising livestock and poultry. Let's cover the basics you need to know about farming so you can start immediately.

- **Prepare the space**

The first step of raising livestock and poultry is preparing the space where you wish to carry out these activities. Whether it's cows, cattle, chickens, or anything you want to raise, they need adequate space that can shield them from the sun and give them the necessary shelter they require.

- **Next is purchasing them**

Look for a good supplier where you can buy healthy livestock, do market research, and ensure the person you choose is reliable and trustworthy.

- **Choose the right food**

The food you feed your livestock depends on the type of animal. Generally, cows eat grass; pigs eat various things, including vegetables and fruits; chickens eat insects and warm, and you can research and check specifically for the food to feed them.

- **Raising livestock animals**

Finally, raising livestock requires careful tending; you can't take care of them and stop after they reach adulthood; it's a nonstop year-round care.

Embracing Permaculture Principles

Permaculture is a low-energy method of growing lots of foods. It contains 12 principles that will give you pointers towards living a sustainable life. You can interpret each principle broadly, so here is a way to apply them to your yard or life.

- Observe and interact: Before taking action, observe and see what is happening. Before you start gardening, observe your space and see which part has the best sun and which has shade. Your job becomes a lot easier when you work in the right spot.
- Catch and store: In a space with abundant resources, it's best to catch and store some. For instance, on rainy days, use gallons and water tanks to save water and store summer vegetables to eat in winter.
- Obtain a yield: Check for yields that will be beneficial for you. Are there uncollected fruits left, or is there some weed from the footpath you can collect for your chickens?

- Apply self-regulation and accept feedback: Climate change can affect your crops, so once this happens, maybe it is Mother Nature trying to tell you to change certain things.
- Use and value renewable resources and services: Use resources that you can reuse again. Instead of black plastic, use cardboard papers and newspapers to suppress weed.
- Produce no waste: Clean and repair your garden tools to use them again instead of throwing them.
- Design from patterns to details: Check which crops you use the most, which path you follow most times, and plant the most valuable plants close to you so you can quickly obtain them when the need arises.
- Integrate rather than segregate: Think of your garden as part of a much wider network of community gardens. You'll benefit from being able to swap your excess produce, sharing your tools, and learning new skills. Rather than trying to achieve self-sufficiency for each household, consider building connections between households and aim for community sufficiency.
- Use small and slow solutions: Instead of going for it at once, plan everything slowly. When building a garden, you can gather many materials cheaply or for free if you're willing to be patient. Going slowly means we save on resources because we won't buy new things that end up wasted.
- Use and value diversity: Eating a diverse range of food keeps us healthy. Growing a diversity of plants means there is always something beneficial for insects to eat and protects your garden from pests and disease.
- Use edges and value the margins: Herbs like nettle and dandelion can forage from the edges of footpaths or unused plots of land.
- Creatively use and respond to change: Human society and nature are continuously changing; think of the changes you need to make that will help you and the community.

6.2 Food Preservation Techniques

Foods are perishable, meaning they can spoil and become useless if we don't preserve them properly. Luckily, there are many ways you can preserve your food naturally. I will discuss some of them with you. So, you must pay attention to details.

Food Preservation Methods

Some of the ways you can preserve your food include:
- **Refrigerating**

The low temperature inside the refrigerator slows down bacterial growth. Chilled foods can be preserved for several days or weeks without getting spoilt.

- **Sugaring**

The sugaring method preserves food by reducing its water content. Sugar can be in granules, sugar syrup, honey, or molasses. Fruits like apples and plums and vegetables like carrots are sugared to make jams or relishes. Sugar and salt can also be added to the brine to preserve certain fish or meats.

- **Salting**

Salt is like sugar; it also draws water out of food items. You can try the salting method with salt and water, then sugar, add the food to the mixture, and put them in cans.

- **Canning**

You must be careful with this method because any mistake can contaminate your food. Ensure the can is airtight and approximate for storing the specific food you want to preserve.

- **Freeze Drying**

In this method, you will first freeze the food under atmospheric pressure, then you come and remove all the water.

- **Vacuum Packing**

This preserves food quality without adding ingredients. Vacuum packing extends the shelf-life of certain foods by sucking out oxygen to limit the growth of microorganisms.

Embracing Pickling and Fermentation

In an era dominated by technology and modern activities, pickling and fermenting can seem a foreign language to many people. However, These traditional food preservation techniques not only offer a nod to our culinary heritage but also bring a host of health benefits and unique flavors to the table.

Pickling is adding acidic liquid like vinegar to food to give it a sour taste. This will help preserve the food. On the other hand, fermentation is when you allow the bacteria in the food to create a sour taste. This will preserve the food and create beneficial probiotics.

Canning Food

If practiced properly, canning is one of the best methods of preserving food. It involves placing foods in jars and heating them to a temperature to destroy the microorganisms that can spoil the food.

Canning methods
Some of the canning methods you can try include;
- Boiling water bath: This is safe for fruits, tomatoes, and pickles. In this method, jars of food are heated by being completely covered with boiling water (212 °F at sea level).
- Atmospheric Steam Canning Method: You must use the steam canner with naturally acidic or properly acidified foods with a pH less than or equal to 4.6. This includes most fruits, preserves, and pickled vegetables. The steam canner is NOT for low-acid foods such as vegetables and meats.
- Pressure Canning Methods: This method suits all kinds of foods like meat, vegetables, etc. Food jars are placed in 2 to 3 inches of water in a pressure canner and then heated to at least 240 °F. This temperature can only be reached in a pressure canner.

How to can your foods
- Gather your food items and wash them thoroughly.
- Prepare the jars and lids.
- You can choose to either raw pack or hot pack the food. In the raw packing method, you will put the raw unheated food directly into the jars, then add hot water or syrup. For the hot packing method, you will heat the food before packing it inside the cans.

6.3 Effective Food Storage

By storing your food properly, you will prevent it from getting spoiled easily, and it will also prevent food burn and other diseases associated with unpreserved food.

What Foods Can You Store?
Some of the foods you can store include:

0-1 years
Dried fruits

1-3 years
Bouillon

Dried pasta
Dark chocolate
Jerky
Oats
Oils
Ramen noodles
Tea
Tomatoes sauce
Jam and jellies

3-4 years
Canned tuna
Pickles
Spices

5-10 years
Canned fruits
Grains
Molasses

10+ years
Instant coffee
Powdered milk
Rice

Forever
Corn starch
Dried beans, lentils and Legumes
Liquor
Maple syrup
Popcorn
Powdered Jell-O
Raw honey
Salt
Soy
Vinegar
Vanilla extract
Sauce
Sugar

Food Storage Containers

There are many types of food storage containers, including glass containers, acrylic containers, brush stainless steel containers, ceramic food storage containers, canisters, etc.

Emergency Food Storage
Store all dry ingredients or supplies off the floor in clean, dry, dark places away from any source of moisture. Foods will maintain quality longer if extreme changes in temperature and exposure to light are avoided.

Grains
Store grains in sturdy 5-gallon food-grade plastic buckets or containers with tight-fitting lids. Cover the wheat with the lid, but not tightly, for five or six hours before tightening the lid to be airtight. Other grains you can store using this method include rye, rice, oats, triticale, barley, and millet.

Non-fat Dry Milk/Dairy Products
You can also store these products in an airtight container. Dry milk may be stored at 70oF for 12 - 24 months.

Other foods ingredients
You can store other food ingredients, like dried beans, peas, lentils, etc., in an airtight container also. However, when you need to use them, open the box carefully so you can it tightly after use.

Tips for Long-Term Food Storage

When you store food items correctly, you will be surprised how long they can last, even after the suggested expiry date. Tips for long-term food storage include:
- Check and discard all expired items from your pantry, wash the pantry with soapy water, and ensure you get rid of dirt, germs, and bacteria.
- Your storage area must be clean, dry, dark, and cool. 50-70 degrees F is the ideal temperature range to keep food fresher for longer. It's ideal to store food in a basement.
- Keep your food away from factors that can easily spoil it, such as heat, moisture, smell, and critters.
- Apply the concept of FIFO - first in, first out. Placing your newest products at the back to ensure you eat the oldest first.
- Ensure your foods are stored in airtight containers.

6.4 Advanced Food Production Strategies

The general concept of being greener is to be in charge of producing your crops and life. This makes life easy and makes you among the top people who are trying to make the world better. Let's look at some advanced food production strategies you can try.

Make Your Greenhouse Garden to Produce Your Food

A greenhouse is a great way to produce your own food all year round. Here are ways to make your own greenhouse and produce your own food:

Step 1: Prepare the tools
The tools you need include
- Framing materials
- Covering materials
- Basic hand tools
- Safety gear
- Drill
- Impact driver
- Framing nailer
- Level
- Miter saw
- Sawhorse
- Table horse
- Scissors
- Landscape fabric
- Gravel
- Concrete (if building a foundation)

Step 2: Decide the kind of greenhouse you want. There are many types of greenhouses you can choose from, including:
- Cold-frame greenhouses: They are the simplest and smallest greenhouses. They are attached to the house side and can only house a small number of plants.
- Attached greenhouses: As their name implies, they are attached to an existing wall. They have a heat source and can share electricity with the building they are attached to.
- Standalone greenhouses: They are usually not close to a wall, so you need to make an electrical connection and provide them with a heat source.

Step 3: Choose your framing material. You must make your greenhouse frame sturdy so it can withstand the weight of the greenhouse structure. You can choose from a variety of materials to frame your greenhouse, such as

- Aluminum: Although expensive, it's among the best because it's rust-resistant, lightweight, and quite strong.
- PVC pipes are the cheapest and the least durable
- Wood: Wood is charming, but untreated timber will rot in damp environments.
- Galvanized steel: This is mainly purchased by commercial users. It's expensive and sturdy and can rust.

Step 4: Choose your covering material

Select the right covering material; some popular options include:

- Clear plastic sheeting: They are lightweight, cheap, and easy to find, but they don't last.
- Hard double-walled plastics: They are more durable.
- Fiberglass: This material is durable, clear, and UV-resistant, but it's not cheap.
- Glass: They are the most beautiful to use, but they have the disadvantages of being expensive and fragile.

Step 5: Choose a location

Choosing the right location is the most important factor that can influence the success of your greenhouse project. Position your greenhouse facing south or southeast to get the maximum amount of sun exposure, even in the wintertime. Choose a place that doesn't have many bushes or trees that can cast a shadow on your plants.

Step 6: Prepare the greenhouse site

There are two ways you can prepare your greenhouse site

- No foundation: If your site has uneven ground, you must level it. This means adding topsoil and evening it out with a rake.
- Foundation: Alternatively, you can dig and build a foundation for your plant. Ensure the ground is even, and ensure the foundation is below the frost line to keep your plants warm during the colder months.

Step 7: Construct the frame

This will depend on what you want to plant. Follow the instructions written your greenhouse plan or DIY greenhouse kit.

Step 8: Add the covering to the frame

For the most of this step, continue following the instructions from your greenhouse plan or DIY greenhouse kit. Use a sealant to seal the covering to the frame and leave some space for ventilation.

Step 9: Add ventilation and temperature control

Get a fan and heater for your greenhouse to improve airflow and heat when necessary.

How to Earn Money With Your Self-Sufficient Farm

There is no better feeling than making your own food and earning money from it. Here are ways you can make money off your land.

- **Sell the meat:** Perhaps you grow livestock and poultry. You can sell the meat yourself, but this might require some legal procedures. So, instead, look for a local butcher to harvest the animal and take it to their butcher store for processing.
- **Sell the eggs or milk:** If your stocks produce milk or lay eggs, you can use some and sell the remaining.
- **Sell the animals:** If you don't plan to sell the meat, you can sell the whole animal, especially to avoid feeding costs.
- **Sell the fur:** This depends on the animal you have. If you have fiber-producing animals like Angora rabbits, alpacas, or goats, you can sheer them and sell the fur.
- **Sell the produce:** Sell the excess of your produce to a grocery store or at the market or a mini CSA (community-supported agriculture- where people pay you a set amount for the month, and you deliver them fresh produce every week).
- **Sell baked goods:** Many people want homemade goods, but they lack the skill and time to make them. So take charge and start selling some baked goods out of your garden.
- **Lease the property:** Perhaps you are not ready to start using your farm, or you feel it's significant for you; you can lease some parts to someone else.

Hunting and Fishing Techniques

Whether passed down through the ages or developed in modern times, these outside-the-box approaches to putting dinner on the table have one thing in common: They work.

- First, check state and local hunting and fishing regulations before you start.
- Spiderweb Kite Fishing: Gather the spiderwebs you fashion into lures and trail them.
- These worm-shaped lures attract strikes from needlefish—whose narrow mouths make them impossible to catch with hooks. When the kite dips, the fishermen haul in the needlefish. The strong web snags the fish's sharp teeth and rough scales— no hook needed. Fishermen use this method in Solomon Island.
- Spearfishing – using the sharp spear attached to the end of a long pole, spearfishing is used to impale fish. This fishing method involves throwing the spear by hand and shooting a spear gun or thrusting.
- Bow fishing – is the oldest form of fishing style. Like spearfishing, which has a sharp end, bow fishing uses arrows and bows to hunt fish instead of a spear.
- Hand fishing – without using any sharp fishing equipment, hand fishing involves catching fish with your bare hands.
- Angling: This involves attaching hooks and lures to a fishing rod to attract fish.
- Beating is the best-known way of hunting in a group. You will be accompanied by a dog who will flush out your prey towards you.

Chapter 7: Off-the-Grid Security and Self-Defense

Living is about being cautious of different and low-probability events that can occur. One of these probabilities is an intruder attack. This intruder can be a human or wild animal. The big question here isn't about whether the intruder can harm you or not; are you safe? Do you have the necessary tools and equipment to keep yourself safe? Well, rest assured, since this book has promised to cover everything regarding off-grid living, in this chapter, we will look at ways you can secure your property, emergency response planning, and basic self-defense techniques you should learn.

7.1 Securing Your Property

Living off the grid is an aspiration for many people seeking self-sufficiency, tranquility, and a sustainable lifestyle. However, despite this peace and freedom, one concern for off-grid leaving is security. Here, we will look at some of the significant strategies to safeguard your home.

- **Understand your environment:** The first line of defense in living off-grid is understanding your environment. Familiarize yourself with the natural terrain, weather patterns, and any wildlife that might pose a threat. This information will help identify security weaknesses and natural deterrents.
- **Physical Barriers and Natural Deterrents:** Fences, gates, and walls are classic deterrents. However, consider using natural barriers like thorny bushes or dense hedges. They blend into the environment and act as barriers to intruders.
- **Use of Renewable Energy Sources for Security Systems:** Generally, off-grid living relies on renewable energy. You can leverage these technologies by using modern security like solar-powered security lights and motion sensors. Aside from being eco-friendly, they function in remote areas without access to the main grid.
- **Surveillance technology:** You can adapt modern surveillance technology into your off-grid living. You can use solar-powered or battery-operated security cameras with remote access to monitor your environment.
- **Safe Storage of Valuables:** Purchase secure storage for your valuables. This can be a reinforced safe room or hidden storage area that will be difficult for invaders to access.
- **Community Networking:** In most remote areas, neighbors rely on each other for survival. So, you must create a good relationship with your neighborhood to help each other in times of need. You can also form or join neighborhood programs.

- **Training and Preparedness:** Train and prepare yourself for emergencies. This includes learning self-defense strategies and keeping first aid boxes, and emergency response kits. Have a well-thought-out emergency plan for off-grid living.
- **Animal Guards:** Animals like dogs can be valuable security assets. They can alert you of the presence of intruders or strangers. Even smaller animals like geese can be surprisingly effective in raising an alarm.
- **Regular maintenance and upkeep:** Inspect and maintain your property regularly. This includes checking fences, gates, and security systems to ensure everything is in working order. Mostly, a well-maintained property is less attractive to intruders.
- **Privacy and Discretion:** Lastly, be mindful of the people you interact with and how much information you share about your property. Publicizing your off-grid lifestyle or valuable assets can make you a target—practice discretion in online and offline conversations.

7.2 Emergency Response Planning

Disaster can happen at any moment, and since you can't always determine when or where it will happen, you must always prepare yourself. It's vital to know how you can respond to any situation by creating an emergency response plan.

To help you get started, here is how to create an emergency response plan for your home:

- **Consider your unique needs.**

Where you live, and your family's specific needs are the factors you should consider in your home emergency plans. Know the kind of natural disaster that can occur in your area and the best way you can prepare for that emergency. Aside from fire, the emergencies that we all know are hurricanes, severe flooding, volcanoes, or tornadoes. Additionally, determine if you need to make specific arrangements for certain family members like those with disabilities, older people, infants, or young children. You should also consider the medical and dietary needs of your house's members.

- **Make a disaster supplies kit.**

A disaster supply kit is a great way to put all your things in one place so that when the necessity to evacuate arises, you will do so without any hassle. Ideally, your kit should fit in one or two easy-to-carry bags and should contain items to help you survive on your own for at least 72 hours. The items you should include in your disaster supplies kit include prescription and medications, glasses, infant formula and diapers, pet food, extra water, cash or traveler check and change, emergency reference material such as a first aid book, sleeping bank, or warm blanket for everyone. Once a year, review the emergency kit, remove what's not necessary, and replace expired items with new supplies.

- **Know where to go.**

Emergencies are different, so your safe place should also vary. First, prepare a space in your home where you will move depending on the emergency. Set a meeting spot outside your home and notify everyone so you all will gather in one place in case of unforeseen situations. Lastly, determine where you will move to in case the need to evacuate arises and plan a simple route that will take you there.

- **Stay connected.**

Create a family communication plan. This plan should include information on how you will receive local emergency alerts (radio, TV, text, etc.), as well as information on how to keep in contact with each other. Ensure every family member has emergency phone numbers saved in their phones and a written contact card that includes police, hospital, a nearby hospital, and an out-of-area emergency contact. You can easily reach someone outside town if there is an emergency in your neighborhood. So, it's good to design an out-of-area contact and notify all your family members to keep in touch so you will know they are safe. Furthermore, if there is a disaster in your area, mark yourself safe on Facebook or register on the American Red Cross Safe and Well website so your loved ones know you're okay.

- **Protect your pets.**

When making your emergency response plan, remember your pets. List some pet-friendly shelters along your evacuation route. Also, remember to include pet emergency items in your disaster management risk.

- **Write it down and practice.**

Ensure you have your emergency response plan written with detailed instructions for each situation. How you react to tornadoes will differ from how you react to evacuation situations. So, you must plan for each. Practice your plans twice a year. For evacuation drills, you should grab your emergency kit and drive to your evacuation route.

- **Review your insurance**

Before any disaster happens, it's good to review your insurance policy with your agent and ensure you have the right to coverage for emergencies. For instance, a standard home policy typically doesn't include protections like flood insurance or earthquake coverage. You also should make sure you know how to file a claim, if necessary, whether through your carrier's loss reporting phone line or website or through your agent.

7.3 Basic Self-Defense Techniques

Are you sure that you can defend yourself whenever intruders attack you? Probably not; the truth is that just because you can handle the toughest workout sessions doesn't mean you can protect yourself and your loved ones in emergencies. Here are some self-defense tips and beginner-friendly moves that will give you the best chance of escape in emergencies:

- **Prevention Can Be the Best Protection**

The first step in self-defense is being aware of your environment; becoming self-aware will make you easily react to the worst case. For instance, only park your car in a well-lit area and ensure you have protective items like a safety whistle and spray or safety necklace.

- **Lock your car doors immediately after you enter**

Although it's easy to name obvious situations in which you might get attacked, there are some non-obvious situations that, unless they happen, you may never think of the possibilities. People, especially women, tend to get into their car and sit for a while pressing the phone, which is a habit that causes trouble. If, unfortunately, a predator is watching you, this is a perfect opportunity they will use to attack you. Mostly, they will get into the passenger's seat, and either harm you or tell you where to go. This is why immediately you enter your car, lock the doors, and leave.

- **Be mindful of drinks around strangers.**

Whenever you attend a party, stick to your friends; if you leave your drink out of sight, even if it's for a few seconds, get a new one. It's very easy to spike a drink with a date rape drug. When going out with someone you aren't very familiar with or when going to an unknown place, notify a family member or friend and remember to always have your phone charged wherever you are.

How to Make a Scene

The second stage of prevention is sounding an alarm. If somebody is trying to harm you or you are in an unfavorable situation, yell, back off, or scream. If you do this, you will attract people's attention and simultaneously alert your predator that you are not an easy target. When you find yourself in such a situation, it's time to get into escape mode. You want to try all possible ways to run and survive.

Remember that you can even escape from someone bigger or stronger than you. The first thing you should do is to scream while trying to escape; if they are already holding you, then you try some defensive moves that will open room for escape.

Know the Most Vulnerable Areas (Yours and Theirs)

For starters, the areas most vulnerable to attack affect seeing and breathing—the eyes, nose, mouth, and throat. You are also more vulnerable when you are on the ground versus standing.

While ending up on the ground while trying to defend yourself is possible, you should try as much as possible to remain standing. Aside from the eyes, nose, and mouth, the groin is another area most vulnerable to a strike.

Basic Self-Defense Moves

Fortunately, you don't necessarily need a black belt in karate to defend yourself. Practice the following self-defense strategies at home frequently until you feel confident you can practice them outside. Self-defense techniques not only make you safer and increase your chances of survival but also increase your confidence and personal power.

- **Ready Stance**

This is best applied when somebody follows you. Use it to set a firm body language boundary. To achieve this position, stand with your feet shoulder-width apart, knees slightly bent, and your weight evenly distributed.

Keep your hands before your face, elbows in, and chin down. Stay relaxed but alert, ready to move or react quickly.

- **Palm-Heel Strike**

This should be your last resort move to create a chance for escape. It's best used when the attacker's face isn't blocked or covered, and you can reach the face by stretching your arms. To execute a palm heel strike, stand with your feet shoulder-width apart, knees slightly bent, and hands up in a defensive position. Raise your dominant hand, keeping your fingers straight together, with the palm facing down. Shift your weight forward onto your front foot. Drive your palm forward and downward, aiming to strike the target with the heel of your palm. Follow through with your strike, keeping your arm slightly bent upon impact to absorb shock and minimize injury to your hand. Quickly retract your hand to the starting position to prepare for further strikes or defensive maneuvers.

- **Front Kick to the Groin**

This last resort move is especially beneficial against a tall person. To do it: Stand with your feet shoulder-width apart, knees slightly bent, and hands up in a defensive position. Lift your dominant knee up towards your chest while keeping your foot flexed, and your toes pointed upward. Extend your leg forward quickly, aiming to strike the target with the ball of your foot or the base of your toes. Aim for the groin area of your opponent, using the upward motion of your kick to generate power. Recoil your leg back to the starting position immediately after the kick to maintain balance and readiness for further action. Remember to practice control and accuracy to ensure effective execution of the technique.

- **Hammerfist Punch**

This is the most effective self-defense technique when used correctly. Here, you will first stand in a stable stance with your feet shoulder-width apart, knees slightly bent, and hands up in a defensive position. Raise your dominant hand, forming a fist with your fingers curled inward and your thumb wrapped tightly around the outside of your fingers. Instead of punching with your knuckles, as in a traditional punch, turn your fist sideways so that the bottom part (the "hammer") makes contact with the target. Keep your wrist straight and your arm slightly bent to absorb shock upon impact. Drive your hammer fist forward and downward with force, aiming to strike the target with the meaty part of your palm below your pinky finger. Follow through with your strike, maintaining control and balance throughout the motion. Quickly retract your arm to the starting position to prepare for further strikes or defensive maneuvers.

Chapter 8: Essential Skills for Off-the-Grid Living

Living off the grid is entirely different from living in town, where you can purchase nearly everything at your convenience and access many essential services. Moreover, many things can break or need repair. Even if you are only a few miles from town, you must equip yourself with basic survival skills. In this chapter, you will explore some essential skills you need to be equipped with, such as first aid and medical skills, survival skills, and DIY repair skills.

8.1 First Aid and Medical Skills

Knowing basic first aid skills could save someone's or your own life. These skills are easy to learn and useful in emergencies. Basic skills like CPR, setting a splint, and stopping bleeding in dire situations are essential.

- **CPR (Cardiopulmonary resuscitation)**

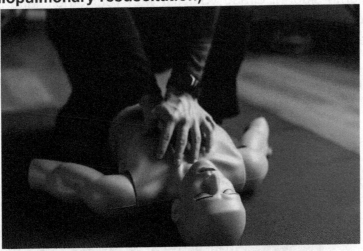

The most well-known survival skill is mostly CPR; learning this procedure is simple and takes only about five minutes to perform. For starters, the steps for CPR include. Opening the airway first, tilt the victim's head slightly, lifting their chin to open it. Check breathing, look, listen, and feel breathing for no more than 10 seconds. If the victim is not breathing normally, proceed to CPR. Perform chest compressions:

- Place the heel of one hand on the center of the victim's chest (between the nipples).
- Place the other hand on top of the first, interlocking your fingers.
- Lean over the victim with your arms straight and press down hard and fast, at least 100-120 compressions per minute.
- Allow the chest to come back up fully between compressions.

Give Rescue Breaths
- Tilt the head back and lift the chin.
- Pinch the nose shut and cover the victim's mouth with yours.
- Give two rescue breaths, each lasting about one second, and watch for the chest to rise.
- If the chest does not rise, reposition the head and try again.

Continue CPR
Perform cycles of 30 chest compressions and two rescue breaths until help arrives or the victim shows signs of life. Only stop if the scene becomes unsafe, you're too exhausted to continue, or if emergency services take over.

Heimlich Maneuver
This is applicable when a person is choking. Stand behind the person choking and wrap your arms around their waist. Make a fist with one hand and place it slightly above the person's navel, thumb side in. Grasp your fist with your other hand and press into the person's abdomen with a quick upward thrust. Repeat thrusts until the object blocking the airway is dislodged or the person becomes unconscious.

- **Set a splint**

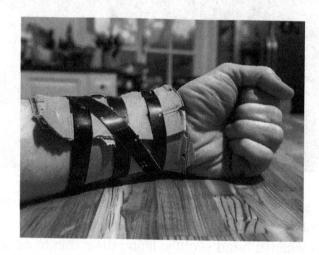

If you are far from help and someone in your group has suffered a broken bone, you'll need to set a splint. You can set a splint with household items. To do this, first check for any obvious deformities, swelling, or signs of broken bones. Next, Gather materials like a padded board, strips of cloth, or a pre-made splint. Support the limb in its current position to prevent further injury. Place the padded board alongside the limb, then secure it with the strips of cloth or bandages. Ensure it's snug but not too tight. Also, make sure the splint isn't cutting off circulation by checking for warmth, color, and pulse below the injury.

- **Treat a Burn**

To treat a burn, which generally depends on its severity, First, tune cool (not cold) water over the burn for 10-15 minutes. Then, gently clean the burn with mild soap and water. Use aloe vera gel or an antibiotic ointment to soothe and protect the burn. Cover the burn with a sterile gauze bandage. Take over-the-counter pain medication if needed. Don't pop any blisters that form.

- **Spot a Concussion**

To spot a concussion, first, check if the person is conscious. If they're unconscious, call emergency services immediately. These may include confusion, headache, dizziness, nausea, vomiting, blurred vision, slurred speech, sensitivity to light or noise, balance problems, memory loss, or changes in behavior. Keep an eye on them for the next few hours, especially if they're a child or an older adult. Look out for any worsening symptoms or signs of complications. Encourage the person to rest both physically and mentally. Avoid activities that worsen symptoms, such as strenuous exercise or screen time.

- **Support a Sprain**

You should wrap the sprain with an ice bandage and elevate it until a doctor can take care of it.

- **Sutures and stitches**

Hopefully, you will never find yourself in a situation that will require sutures or stitches because mostly this requires knowledge and practice.

8.2 Survival Skills

Living off the grid requires essential skills to ensure safety and security. Let's look at some essential skills to thrive off-grid living.

- **Locating and Harvesting Water**

One of the essential skills for off-grid living is learning how to locate, harvest, and treat water. If you don't have access to traditional water sources, it's crucial to look for alternative methods of getting clean water. We have already discussed harvesting water. Now, let's so look at ways to locate water in an off-grid setting. For sourcing water, it is better to purchase a plot with a borehole or well on the land. If there is one nearby, you could contact the owner to use their water source for a small fee. A third option would be to see if your land would benefit from digging your borehole. Traditionally, you can source your water from rivers, streams, or any natural source; most times, unless the water is contaminated by external force, it's always clean and doesn't require much treatment.

- **Preparing food**

Hunger can kill. Without food, it will be hard to survive, and since you are living off-grid, perhaps you will be in charge of preparing your food. This is an essential skill that you need to learn. Ensure you have a cast-iron skillet, a Dutch oven, a hand-crank mixer, and a manual can opener. Aside from preparing the food, you must learn how to cook it. One popular cooking method is firewood, a stove, or an oven, which all can be used to cook various foods.

- **Laundry**

Another vital skill to learn is laundry; there are various methods to clean your clothes. You can wash them using your hands by immersing them in soapy water, or you can use a brush or scrub to wash your clothes.

- **Food preservation**

The importance of food preservation skills can never be overemphasized. Fortunately, we have discussed methods to preserve your food to last years without spoiling it. For a quick recap, some food preservation methods include canning, salting, freeze-drying, etc.

- **Hygiene and sanitation**

Maintaining a clean environment doesn't only ensure that your home remains clean but also reduces the risk of developing diseases. Plan and prepare with the necessary tools and supplies to maintain cleanliness. Other personal hygiene practices include regular bathing and hand washing.

- **Handling sewage**

Without a proper way to dispose of sewage, the disease will spread. So it's necessary to ensure that you have a proper method of handling and disposing of waste. Mostly, in an off-grid setting, the toilet is either a non-pump septic system, a composting toilet, an outhouse, or a "dry toilet" system.

- **Classes**

Educate yourself on basic survival skills by attending programs to provide this knowledge. You can do so online and offline, depending on your convenience.

- **Be familiar with herbal medicines**

Herbal medicines usually come in handy, especially in emergencies. You need to know the uses of each so you can apply them properly. For instance, Echinacea can be taken as a tea to treat the common cold; Ginseng can be taken as a tea or in powdered form as an anticancer and antidiabetic agent. Ginkgo can be used for the treatment of different illnesses such as cardiovascular disease, dimential, neurological problems, and sexual dysfunction. Elderberry has long been used to relieve headaches, nerve pain, toothaches, colds, viral infections, and constipation. Historically, St. John's wort was used to help with wound healing and provide a relief from ailments like insomnia, depression, kidney and respiratory tract disease. Today, it's primarily prescribed to treat mild to moderate depression. Turmeric, popularly known as spice, can treat various conditions, including chronic inflammation, pain, metabolic syndrome, and anxiety. Ginger is used for relieving nausea associated with pregnancy, chemotherapy, and medical operations. Sometimes referred to as "nature's Valium," valerian is used to treat anxiety and insomnia.

8.3 DIY Repair Skills

Owning a home is great, but it comes with many responsibilities. While we can't help you with how you can arrange things around your house, we can at least help you with the skills to repair them when they are damaged.

- **How to Repair Drywall**

Drywalls can be damaged in many ways. Starting from hanging pictures to children or pets scratching it. Luckily, repairing drywall is an easy project that, when done, can make a huge difference in your home's appearance.

All you need is a utility knife, sandpaper, a putty knife, joint compound, and extra drywall. Using your utility knife, cut the damaged area out of the wall. Use the piece to trace an appropriately sized drywall from the extra. This is your drywall patch. Apply joint compound around the patch's edges, slide it into the wall, and let it dry overnight. The next day, and the excess joint compound to flush with the wall. Sand it smoothly, paint it, and you're done!

- **How to Remove Wallpaper**

Whether you have wallpaper you are tired of seeing or buy a house whose wallpaper doesn't suit your taste, here is a simple method to remove it without damaging your wall. To remove wallpaper, purchase a scoring tool (available at most hardware stores). This will perforate the outermost layer of the wallpaper, allowing the following solution to soak in. Mix a solution of ¼ parts liquid fabric softener with ¾ parts hot water. This mixture will reactivate the adhesive on the wallpaper, making it easier to pull off. Apply this solution with a sprayer, let it sit for 3-5 minutes, and scrape the wallpaper off with a putty knife. If you still have leftover adhesive on your wall once the paper is gone, repeat the process until everything is clean.

- **How to Fix a Leaky Sink**

To fix a leaky sink, sometimes you need to tighten the nut around the pipe. If it's a severe issue, inspect the component and check for cracks or stripped metal threads; if there are one, replace them, and your problem is solved.

- **How to Unclog Drains**

Every drain clogs, so it's essential to know how to unclog it to save yourself the hassle of hiring a plumber. To do this, first pour half a cup of baking soda onto the drain, followed by half a cup of vinegar. Cover the drain using a stopper or plunger and let it sit for 15 minutes if there are stubborn clogs; you need to repeat the process a few times.

- **How to Caulk**

When the caulk around your sink, window, or tub starts degrading, it's time to replace it so the seal will remain intact. With just a tube of caulk, a caulk gun, and a few essential tools, you can fix it quickly. The basic process is: remove the old caulk, tape the area off, apply the new caulk, smooth it, and let it dry.

- **How to replace shower head**

To replace your shower head, begin by removing the old one. First, turn it counterclockwise with your hands or pliers for a firmer grip. Then, clean any dirt, debris, or residues on the shower arm thread. Next, install the new showerhead following the manufacturer's guide.

- **How to Prune Shrubs and Bushes**

Even if your yard is small, you will need to prune the shrubs and bushes from time to time to avoid the growth of unwanted plants or attracting wild animals to your yard. Cut them with pruning shears before you address any trimming or shaping with live branches. It's best to do this in late fall and early spring optimally, but maintenance can be performed whenever you have time or need.

- **How to Hang a Picture**

Pictures can add vibrant color to your home and make it more welcoming to visitors. Fortunately, pictures are easy to hang; you only need a pencil, hammer, and nail. Consider hanging your pictures around eye level. If you're going for a gallery wall, lay out the design so the pictures in the center are either at eye level or slightly above or below it. Lightly mark the spot where your nail or nails will go with your pencil. A heavy picture will require heavy nails, while the light ones can be easily hanged using light nails. Check the weight of your picture and decide which nail will go best with it before drilling it on the wall.

- **How to Mow the Lawn**

If you have never had a mow or lawn before, this might sound like an intimidating task but believe that as long as you have the necessary tools, you will find it an enjoyable and rewarding task. Begin by trimming up the edges of your lawn and around hard-to-mow places like your mailbox and planters. This will save you the headache of maneuvering the mower around those spaces and prevent potential damage. After that, your lawn mower can care for most of your yard. Once you get into a routine, mowing once a week or every other week, ensure you don't mow in the same pattern. By changing the direction you mow your lawn, you'll reduce turf wear, meaning your lawn will look better in the long run.

Chapter 9: Off-the-Grid Transport and Communication

In today's digital era, transportation and staying connected are taken for granted. We rely on the internet or our smartphones to get in touch with our loved ones, but there will be situations where that won't work. It won't work when you are in a remote area without access to a network or modern transportation means. This is why it's necessary to equip yourself with the knowledge of both modern and traditional means of communication and transportation. So, in whichever situation you find yourself in, it will come in handy. In this chapter, you will explore off-the-grid communication and transportation methods.

9.1 Off-Grid Transportation

In today's modern settings, where environmental concerns and self-sufficiency are increasing, off-grid transportation methods offer a valuable solution. Off-grid transportation methods don't rely on fossil fuels or centralized infrastructure. Instead, they depend on renewable energy, such as solar systems or human power, to provide humans the freedom to travel.

There are many reasons you should choose off-grid transportation means: they offer environmental sustainability, are cost-effective, provide health and fitness, and independence and freedom. Some other benefits of these transportation methods include reducing carbon footprint, enhancing personal well-being, and simplifying urban commutes.

Types of off-grid transportation

There is a wide range of off-grid transportation, each with unique features and benefits.

- **Bicycles**

Bicycles are a simple and efficient mode of transportation. They are powered by human energy, making them eco-friendly and healthy. Whether you are going for short distances or long distances, a bicycle can be your buddy to accompany you on your travels. Moreover, they are cheap, and even if you don't know how to use them, you only require a 24-48 hours lesson to grab the basics.

- **Electric Scooters**

Electric scooters have gained more popularity in recent years. Rechargeable batteries power them and offer a practical and emission-free mode of transportation for shorter distances.

- **Skateboards**

Recently, companies have manufactured electrical versions of skateboards, providing a fun and engaging way to travel short distances. This offers an amazing riding experience, especially for being environmentally friendly.

- **Electric Unicycles**

These modes of transportation combine portability and maneuverability, making them the best for urban transportation. They have improved battery technology that offers reliable and eco-friendly transportation options.

- **Electric Vehicles**

The automobile industry has changed thanks to electric cars, which provide a sustainable substitute for conventional gasoline-powered vehicles. They help to lessen air pollution, use rechargeable batteries, and have zero tailpipe emissions.

- **Solar-Powered Vehicles**

Solar panels are used in solar-powered automobiles to collect solar energy and transform it into electrical power. These cars offer long-distance drivers an independent power source and are environmentally beneficial.

- **Horses**

Horses are still a practical off-grid transportation option, having been utilized for millennia. They offer a distinctive and entertaining riding experience, are environmentally sustainable, and run on neither electricity nor fuel. In remote locations or for trail riding, where access to infrastructure and roadways may be restricted, horses are especially well-suited.

- **Alternative Fuel Cars**

Alternative fuel vehicles, like biodiesel vehicles, are an additional off-grid mobility option to consider. Fuels from renewable sources, including plant or animal fats, are used in these vehicles. As a more environmentally friendly option to conventional petrol or diesel vehicles, biodiesel has lower emissions and can work with diesel engines.

Factors to Consider When Choosing Off-Grid Transportation

Here are some factors you should consider when selecting an off-grid transportation mode.

- Distance and Terrain: Consider the distance and the kind of terrain you will be traversing frequently. This will assist you in selecting a vehicle that meets your needs and has the requisite range and capacity.
- Infrastructure and Charging Facilities: Think about the infrastructure needed for your selected off-grid transportation alternative or the accessibility of charging

stations. Make sure there are enough amenities to meet your needs while traveling.

- Safety Features: When selecting an off-grid vehicle, put safety first. To guarantee a safe ride, look for strong brakes, sturdy construction, and adequate illumination.
- Cost and Accessibility: Establish your spending limit and evaluate the total cost of ownership, considering upkeep, charging expenses, and any other accessories or safety equipment needed.
- Local Laws: Learn about the rules and restrictions in your area about off-grid driving. Specific transit modes, speed limits, and insurance and license requirements may apply in some areas.

9.2 Off-Grid Communication

Here are five reliable and realistic off-grid communication methods that let you have a conversation like you would on a cell phone when your cell is down:

- **Ham radio**

Regarding off-grid communication, only a few will match the power of ham radio, also called amateur radios. Ham radios work by transmitting and receiving signals through antennas. Their communication range varies depending on frequency, antenna height, atmospheric conditions, and obstacles like buildings or terrain. In an ideal condition, you can use a ham radio to communicate with people 100 miles from you. These devices are beneficial in emergencies as they provide a means of staying connected during natural disasters in the wilderness. Note that to operate a ham radio legally, you need to obtain a license and some technical knowledge. In off-grid settings where modern communication methods might be ineffective, ham radio is a worthy means of communication.

- **CB radio**

If you are looking for a simple and accessible option, CB radio is your best option. Citizens Band radio, or CB radio, operates on 40 channels and does not require a license. It offers a reliable means of communication in local areas. The people mostly using CB radios are truck drivers, outdoor enthusiasts, and emergency responders.

It transmits and receives radio signals using handheld devices or vehicle-mounted units. However, compared to ham radios, their range is shorter, and they will only reach a few miles, though they are still effective off-grid communication methods.

- **Satellite Phone:**

When you are in a remote area without a network, a satellite phone can rescue you. They connect to orbiting satellites to provide global coverage, enabling you to make calls and send messages anywhere.

Whether you're exploring remote regions or facing emergencies in areas lacking traditional infrastructure, satellite phones become invaluable tools for staying connected. But keep in mind that satellite phones are more expensive than others, still their ability makes them a worthy investment.

- **Walkie Talkie**

This is an amazing portable and off-grid solution that you can use. They are handled devices that provide short-range communications through radio waves. They are easy to use and don't require many legal procedures. Walkie-talkies work by transmitting and receiving radio signals between two or more devices. The range of communication for walkie-talkies typically varies based on factors such as terrain, obstacles, and the power of the devices.

Overall, if you are looking for a communication device to exchange information within a short mile, a talkie can bridge that gap. Walkie-talkies are commonly used by hikers, campers, and event organizers, enabling quick and reliable communication in off-grid situations.

- **Mesh Networking Devices:**

When traditional infrastructure is unavailable, mesh networking devices establish connections where none exist. Devices like goTenna or Sonnet create peer-to-peer networks, forming a web of interconnected devices.

They create a decentralized network by linking multiple devices together, with each device acting as a "node" or connection point that can directly communicate with nearby devices. Remember that the mesh networking range depends on the number of similar devices in the neighborhood. These devices are perfect to use in places where communication is difficult due to lack of infrastructure.

Two "One Way Street" Options

Sometimes, off-grid communication is about sending or receiving critical information, meaning it's not all about conversation. Two options can fit this scenario: shortwave radios and GPS messenger beacons.

Shortwave radios: Allows you to deliver up-to-the-minute in emergencies. One perfect example is the case of the Maui fires; lack of communication left people without a way to be in touch with their loved ones, and vital cell phone alerts were undelivered. In this case, shortwave radios can be used to save lives.

GPS messenger beacons: An alternative to shortwave radios is the GPS messenger beacons. It enables you to send distress signals and your precise coordinates to rescue services. This allows for quick and targeted assistance in emergencies, even when direct communication seems impossible.

Chapter 10: Thriving Off-the-Grid

Off-grid living can be the right choice if you're seeking complete freedom! Living off the grid entails being disconnected from public facilities such as electrical, water, and sewage. It typically entails leading a self-sufficient, efficient, and minimalist lifestyle. Even though setting things up can be difficult, you can create a completely self-sufficient homestead with diligence and the appropriate tools and thrive. In this chapter, you will discover ways you can overcome off-the-grid challenges, how you can find fulfillment in self-sufficiency, and tips for long-term sustainability.

10.1 Overcoming Challenges

Off-grid living is a topic you may have encountered if you have ever read about living off the land and escaping the madness of contemporary life. Over 200,000 Americans have decided to live off the grid to live more sustainably. Living off the grid might have a high learning curve. However, like every endeavor has challenges, off-grid living also has some. In this subchapter, we will unveil some of the challenges of living off-grid and how you can overcome them.

- **Location, Location, location**

Location isn't only a problem for urban settlers but also for off-gridders. Many suburban areas won't let you live in communities without utilities, which means you need to find land that is rural and legal enough to live freely without legal consequences. Consider the amount of land you will need to live a sustainable life and think of the things you want to do on your land and the size of your family. You will also need to stay near the water source since you will be responsible for water harvesting.

- **Power Source**

Another challenge of living off-grid you might encounter is looking for a power source. Although you can live completely without a power source by depending on the sun, you do all the necessary things you need to do in the afternoon and rest from evening through the night. But still, having a power source makes living a lot easier. Most off-gridders opt for a solar energy system because it is generally considered the best long-term investment. However, if you are on a tight budget and can't afford a solar system, you can consider other alternatives. Check your current power bill to see how much energy you consume, and use this as a baseline for the type of energy setup you need. Once your power source is established, you may be consuming more energy than you have available. To help conserve energy, only run one appliance at a time and try to do so during daylight hours to maximize solar energy. Use a wood stove for cooking and gas for the stovetop rather than electricity.

- **Sourcing Food**

Producing your own food is another highlight of living off-grid living. Create a kitchen garden in your home, which you can slowly expand later. One of the biggest challenges in sourcing food, which often happens at the beginning, is finding a variety of balanced diets. While you can depend on fruits and other things, you might need to eat solid foods sometimes to survive. Not all homesteaders can raise livestock within their first years of off-grid living. So, you might need to depend on other food sources like trading some of the things you have and are valuable to others for food. To also solve food problems, you must learn to cook and preserve food to have enough food during the season when your garden is less productive. Hunting is another valuable skill useful for off-grid living.

- **Water supply**

A close and reliable water supply is vital. Without water, there will be no life because you can't harvest, you can't raise livestock, you can't do any domestic activities. Of course, it might be difficult to find land with abundant freshwater sources, so what most off-grid people do is bore a well and use hand pumps to draw water. One of the things that newcomers usually miss the most is running water. Still, if you have a generator, you can have some running water available for a limited period—as long as you don't mind paying for diesel. If you don't have self-composting toilets, installing a greywater system that uses kitchen and laundry wastewater to irrigate the garden and flush the toilet is an excellent method to recycle your water and ensure plenty of it. Whether you have the right to utilize the water on your land is the last issue you might need to consider when it comes to water. In general, you are allowed to use any water source that is on your land for personal use. To ensure you have the legal right to access the water, though, speak with a lawyer before buying your land if you need it for crops or cattle.

- **Time Management**

Living off the grid requires labor equal to several full-time jobs. To make sure everything goes as smoothly as possible, you need excellent time management skills. Off-grid living does not allow for procrastination. Substantial harvests must be stored for the winter, seeds must be grown in season, animals must be fed and milked regularly, and fences and shelter are necessary to keep predators out. Finding enough time daily means you must become an early riser. And to fully enjoy your homestead living, you must plan months or sometimes years ahead. Keep a detailed record of the season, weather change, harvest time, and livestock's birth rates.

- **Budget**

Do you know that choosing to live simply doesn't necessarily mean cheap living? Living off the grid is often romanticized, causing newcomers to forget the significant upfront investment and the continuous cost of raising livestock and growing crops.

Setting up your power source is the major cost you will encounter; depending on your family size, land, home, and activities, you will need at least fifteen to thirty solar panels and a backup power plan, and this can incur tens or thousands of dollars. If you can make this large investment, taking small steps is the best solution. Begin by cooking and growing your food, reduce your carbon footprint by adopting the no-waste policy, and become mindful of your energy consumption. Taking small steps before reaching a breakthrough can help you save money, time, and resources, and you might appreciate things more.

- **Isolation**

The last and most challenging aspect of off-grid living is isolation, especially when you are used to human interactions around you. But on the positive side, living off-grid is a way to escape the hustle and bustle of living in the city. Moreover, you aren't the only one who chooses this living method. So, you might come together with other greeners and create a small community of like-minded people. You can find a lot of off-grid community groups online. You can search for people living in your area and establish a relationship with them so you can exchange goods and services. Experience off-gridders can also give you pointers on how to harvest and, sow and find local vets for your animals.

10.2 Finding Fulfillment in Self-Sufficiency

Off-grid systems aligned with environmental stewardship principles. By depending on sustainable and clean energy sources, they lessen their environmental impact and lower carbon footprints. This environmentally friendly strategy promotes environmental responsibility and aids in preserving natural resources.Living off the grid allows people and communities to prosper in isolation. Since centralized utilities are primarily unavailable in local and remote areas, off-grid living guarantees a steady power supply as long as you power your home with a power source. Off-grid systems are very adaptable to specific requirements. Be it a desert home or a lodge buried away in the mountains, off-grid solutions can be customized to take advantage of the unique energy resources accessible in each place. Its adaptability enables it to be used in a variety of settings. Among the core benefits of off-grid living is a decrease in energy costs. While the first investment might be significantly huge, the long-term benefits you will enjoy are substantial. Energy bills will be the talk of the past; you will enjoy financial freedom and stability.

Off-grid promotes self-reliance and encourages the will to develop essential skills and knowledge. You will learn how to manage your energy system and troubleshoot common issues; self-sufficient living can be empowering and fulfilling. Off-grid communities create a tight-knit bond based on shared values and respecting each other. Residents come together to help each other, support, and share knowledge. This benefit encourages people to live off-grid as they will have fun together and face challenges together.

10.3 Tips for Long-Term Sustainability

We make decisions in life every day that have an impact on the climate, the ecosystem, and other species. There are numerous things we can do to "choose wild" and lessen our environmental imprint, making more space for wild plants and animals. These include what we eat and how many kids we choose to have. Here are some tips for long-term sustainability.

- **Think twice before making any purchase**

Some of the things you purchase can leave an impact on the environment. Even if you can recycle or eliminate it at the end of its life, the damage has already been done. So before you purchase, ask yourself how important that thing is. Do you need it? Opt for a second hand instead of new and purchase products from low impact-impacts.

- **Ditch plastic and switch the reuse**

Plastic never gets away; around 14 million of plastic gets into the ocean every year, making up 80% of marine dirt. Annually, thousands of seabirds, sea turtles, seals, and other aquatic animals are killed due to plastic disposed of into the ocean. You can start removing plastic simply: first, use reusable bags when you shop, and ditch using single-use water bottles, straws, and bags. Avoid using anything packaged in plastic, as every piece of plastic you avoid can significantly change the world.

- **Take extinction off your plate.**

One of the sectors that harm the environment the most on Earth is the meat industry, which uses much water, pollutes the environment, emits greenhouse gases, and destroys habitats. Choosing to consume less meat and eat a greater amount of plant-based foods might thereby lessen your environmental impact. Moreover, the single biggest category of waste dumped in municipal landfills is food. In the US, over 40% of consumable food is wasted, along with all of the water, land, and other natural resources used in its production. So, you need to ensure that you consume the food you buy and shop wisely to avoid food waste.

- **Simplify holidays**

Celebrations such as weddings, birthdays, and holidays can result in needless excess. For instance, Americans produce 23% more waste in December than in other months.

But the issue extends beyond the excess garbage. Because of the fossil fuels, forests, and other natural resources used to manufacture decorations, wrapping paper, crockery, and gifts, wildlife and their habitat are deprived of light during human celebrations. However, you can change your festivities to honor the environment—land, sea, and wildlife. For your upcoming holiday celebration, consider using reusable dinnerware, homemade or used gifts, and foraged plants as decorations instead of plastic décor, extravagant presents, and single-use food and drink containers.

- **Choose organic**

Organic products lessen your influence on the environment and wildlife, whether coffee or fruit. Each year, almost 2 billion pounds of pesticides are marketed in the US. The survival and recovery of hundreds of listed species are threatened by the widespread use of pesticides in fish and wildlife habitats. In addition to contaminating our food, pesticides harm the soil, water, and air. If you garden, cultivate organically to stay away from pesticides at home. By cultivating native, pollinator-friendly plants and eliminating invasive species, you may create a wildlife habitat in your yard to draw beneficial insects and deter harmful pests. By choosing organic, you safeguard your family, vulnerable communities, agricultural workers, wildlife, and the environment by preventing dangerous chemicals from entering our land and water.

- **Ditch fast fashion and animal-based textiles.**

The fast fashion industry is gaining recognition and growing rapidly in recent years. New garments have doubled annually over the last 20 years, and global fashion consumption has increased by 400%. Wool and other animal-based textiles are to blame for various wildlife injuries, extensive habitat loss due to deforestation, and water contamination. Reduce the speed at which you change clothes by taking care of them, fixing them when you can, and buying used or participating in clothing exchanges when you need new clothes. If you must buy new, steer clear of the greenwashing and pick long-lasting brands of clothes manufactured from sustainable materials like Tencel or organic cotton.

- **Be water-wise.**

Given the increasing strain on the world's water resources due to population growth and severe droughts, water conservation is essential. By replacing leaking toilets, taking shorter showers, and selecting low-flow and low-water appliance options, you can save water.

Take into consideration xeriscaping your yard, a landscaping approach that makes use of natural, drought-tolerant plants that need less water and upkeep over time and offer food and habitat for bees and birds.

Additionally, cutting back on meat and dairy items in your diet will help you save water because animal husbandry is one of the major users of water.

- **Boycott products that endanger wildlife.**

In the United States, products made from endangered wildlife are boycotted and prohibited to purchase. However, even if an animal is not listed, using products made from them can harm their species. To avoid contributing to this harmful endeavor, buy conscientiously and select products made from sustainable materials.

- **Fight for the right to choose when and if to start a family.**

With over 8 billion people on Earth, the demand for food, water, land, and fossil fuels pushes other species to extinction. The human population is one of the crises the earth faces. By advocating reproductive health rights and gender equality, you will improve the health of people and the world because the upcoming generation will be less, which means better access to quality education and resources. To get started, talk about family planning with your partner and create a group in your community that advocates the importance of family planning.

Conclusion

I must commend your commitment and intentionality for wanting to lead a life of freedom, resilience, and self-sufficiency. And I trust this book has added some value to you.

To sum up everything, I believe "No Grid Survival Projects Book" is more than just a guide—it's a roadmap to a resilient, self-sufficient lifestyle. With this book, you must have learned the fundamental principles of off-grid living, from understanding what it means to be off-grid to mastering essential skills for survival.

In the chapters of this book, we talked about self-sufficiency, covering everything from energy and water management to food production, shelter construction, and security. We also discussed the benefits and challenges of off-grid living, helping you set realistic goals and develop a comprehensive plan tailored to your needs and resources.

By embracing the DIY spirit and implementing the projects and strategies outlined in this book, you're not just preparing for emergencies or recessions—you're creating a sustainable way of life that fosters independence, resilience, and harmony with the environment.

As you plan to start your off-grid journey, remember that challenges may arise, but with knowledge, preparation, and perseverance, you can overcome them. Stay adaptable, continue learning, and find fulfillment in the freedom and self-reliance that off-grid living offers.

On this note, I thank you for walking with me on this exploration of self-sufficiency and off-grid living. May your path be filled with abundance, resilience, and thriving off the grid.

Also, I will be glad if you can leave your honest review. This will enhance the visibility of this book and help other enthusiasts make informed decisions.

Best wishes for your off-grid adventure!

Stay strong and have fun.

Made in United States
Orlando, FL
22 July 2024

49399959R00052